CW00419827

THE
LITTLE
BOOK
OF
DEVON

JOHN VAN DER KISTE

First published 2011
Reprinted with revisions in 2014
Reprinted 2016

The History Press
The Mill, Brimscombe Port
Stroud, Gloucestershire, GL5 2QG
www.thehistorypress.co.uk

British Library Cataloguing in Publication Data.
A catalogue record for this book is available from the British Library.

ISBN 978 0 7524 6167 0

Typesetting and origination by The History Press
Printed in Turkey by Imak.

CONTENTS

ACKNOWLEDGEMENTS

I can claim to be a Devonian not by birth, as my mother was, but by virtue of having lived in the county since I was barely three years old. Some half a century after being brought here, in assembling the present volume I have thoroughly relished the task of trawling through a variety of sources including books, pamphlets, old newspapers and journals, websites, and last but not least my admittedly less than perfect memory.

I would like to acknowledge my debt in particular to Brian Moseley's Plymouth Data, Derek Tait's Plymouth Local History, Tim Sandles's Legendary Dartmoor, and David Cornforth's Exeter Memories, all online; the vast collection of books I have used in my researches, particularly W.G. Hoskins' magisterial *Devon*, a title no county enthusiast should be without; my wife Kim, for her ever-helpful reading of the draft manuscript prior to publication; and to my publishers at The History Press.

In conclusion, this book is dedicated to Kim and to the memory of my parents Kate and Guy.

John Van der Kiste, 2011

1

ROYALTY & POLITICS

ROYAL DEVON

William the Conqueror
William I came to Exeter in or around March 1068. The city
had been the home of Gytha, mother of King Harold who had
been defeated and killed at the Battle of Hastings in 1066, and
the people rebelled against William, not only because of their
allegiance to her, but also because the Normans were demanding
high taxes to which they objected. When the king and his army
arrived at the city gates they found their way barred, and they laid
siege to it for eighteen days until the citizens gave in and agreed
to make peace. The king conceded, and allowed Gytha to go
into peaceful exile. As part of the settlement he built Rougemont
Castle, so named because of the hill of red earth on which it stood.
Exeter and Okehampton, also the site of a castle, were left in
charge of his henchman Baldwin de Redvers, whom he appointed
Sheriff of Devon.

Catherine of Aragon
As far as historical records show, Princess Catherine of Aragon
was the next member of royalty to visit Devon. In October 1501
she sailed from Spain to England to become the bride of Arthur,
Prince of Wales, the eldest son of King Henry VII. She landed at the
Barbican, and in the words of one effusive contemporary scribe,
'had she been the saviour of the world, she could not have had a
more enthusiastic welcome.' She went to St Andrew's Church to
give thanks for the safe ending of a stormy and unpleasant voyage,

then stayed in a local merchant's house before going to London for her wedding in November. Prince Arthur had always been sickly and he died in April 1502 of what was referred to as the 'sweating sickness'. She remained in England as a widow, and a few weeks after the new Prince of Wales ascended the throne as King Henry VIII, they were married. Her one surviving daughter later became Queen Mary ('Bloody Mary'), but after she repeatedly failed to give the king a living son and heir, Henry divorced Catherine and she died in 1536.

Princess Henrietta Anne

Henrietta Anne, youngest daughter of King Charles I and Queen Henrietta Maria, was the only child of a reigning English sovereign ever born in Devon. In the summer of 1644, during the Civil War, the queen had been in Oxford, but parliamentary forces were building up in the area and it was thought advisable for her to seek safety elsewhere, especially as she was expecting a child. In May she reached Exeter and stayed at Bedford House, where the princess was born on 16 June. In order to avoid capture, the queen left the city two weeks later for France, leaving the child in the care of a lady-in-waiting, Lady Dalkeith. The princess was baptised in Exeter Cathedral on 21 July. King Charles arrived in the city later that week, and the city fathers made large gifts of money to him, the Prince of Wales and various royal officials as an expression of loyalty. A grateful king knighted the mayor, Hugh Crocker.

Charles II

During the reign of King Charles II, the Royal Citadel at Plymouth was built. Unlike most of the West Country, Plymouth had been strongly pro-Cromwell during the Civil War, but their disillusion with the Commonwealth set in after Cromwell's death and an acute shortage of money which resulted in the seamen not being paid. However, the restoration of the monarchy was seen as a possible return to better times for the town. This coincided with disputes between Holland and France, and in 1665 it was decided to construct a fortress on Plymouth Hoe for defence purposes. The king's main reason for building the Citadel was ostensibly because he recognised the strategic importance of Plymouth as a coastal town when it came to war on England's enemies, though it was believed for some years that he had been angered by the town's unfriendly attitude towards his father and therefore sought some kind of revenge, or at least wished to 'overawe' the town as well as his foes across the Channel, although there is no firm evidence to support this view.

The king paid at least one visit to the area during its construction. Above the gateway in Hoe Road is the royal coat of arms supported by a lion and a unicorn, and the date 1670, with a tablet inscribed, '*Carolus Secundus Dei Gratiae Magnae Britanniae Franciae at Hiberniae Rex*' (British sovereigns did not formally relinquish the style of King of France until the Act of Union in 1801). It had always been intended that a statue of the king would be placed there, but there is some doubt as to whether such a work of art was ever completed.

William III

During the 'Glorious Revolution', William, Prince of Orange, landed at Brixham on 5 November 1688, an invasion which culminated in he and his wife Mary replacing her unpopular father, King James II, on the throne. On their first night there, some of his soldiers found billets in the local cottages, though he himself made do with a mattress on the floor of a fisherman's hut. After spending a night at Paignton, they entered Exeter on their march towards London on 9 November. Four weeks later James abdicated, throwing the Great Seal into the Thames as he fled into exile, and William and Mary became joint sovereigns in his place.

George III and his family

Since the reign of King George III, every British sovereign has visited Devon at least once, though in some cases not necessarily after they ascended to the throne. George III, Queen Charlotte and their eldest daughters, Princesses Charlotte, the Princess Royal Augusta, and Elizabeth, came to Plymouth in the summer of 1789. They stayed at Saltram House, and during their few days in the area they visited the town's new theatre in George Street, named the Theatre Royal in the king's honour. He also visited a new dock which was then under construction, the Citadel and the Victualling Office. The most spectacular event of their visit was a review of the fleet and a mock naval battle in the Sound, with about a hundred ships taking part.

Three years earlier, in March 1786, Prince William Henry, the king's third son, who had joined the Royal Navy, was initiated as a Freemason at the Prince George Inn, Vauxhall Street, and later that year he was given the Freedom of Plymouth. After naval service in the Americas he returned to the town, and lodged for a while at a merchant's house. In 1788 his two elder brothers, George, Prince of Wales, later King George IV, and Frederick, Duke of York, came down to see him, paying duty visits to the Citadel, the dockyard, and Mount Edgcumbe, when not sampling the best high life that the town had to offer, or as contemporaries eloquently said, 'painting the town red'.

In 1789 Prince William was persuaded to threaten to stand for election to parliament as member for Totnes, as a protest against the delay in his father giving him a title. Had he tried to persist, an election of the king's son would probably have been invalid, but he duly got his title, that of Duke of Clarence. Although he never visited Devon during his short reign, the Royal William Victualling Yard, Stonehouse, which was named in his honour, was completed in 1835. The gateway was later surmounted by a large statue of the king.

Queen Victoria

Queen Victoria paid several visits to Devon. She was only a baby of seven months in December 1819 when she and her parents, the Duke and Duchess of Kent, came to stay at Woolbrook Glen, Sidmouth, arriving in a snowstorm on Christmas Day. The duke, like most of his family, was inclined to be a spendthrift; Sidmouth was far away from his creditors, and it would be a very inexpensive place to live. The previously hale and hearty duke, who often boasted that he would outlive all his brothers, went walking along the cliffs during a storm the next month, before returning to the house and sitting by the fire without changing his soaking wet boots; he caught a severe chill which turned into pneumonia and died on 23 January 1820, aged fifty-two. The house has since become the Royal Glen Hotel, and a plaque on the wall refers to the family's visit which ended in such sadness.

In July 1833, as fourteen-year-old heiress to the throne, Victoria and the Duchess of Kent stopped at Plymouth on a cruise along the south coast, and Princess Square was later named in her honour.

In August 1843 the queen, Prince Albert and their court took the royal yacht *Victoria and Albert* on its maiden voyage while paying a visit to King Louis-Philippe of France. On their way they enjoyed a cruise along the south coast of England, and put in at Plymouth Sound. They received deputations from the Corporations of Plymouth and Devonport on board, and Prince Albert was invested with the office of Lord High Steward. Later that day they visited the dockyard, from where carriages took them for a drive at a foot's pace all over the Three Towns. The streets were so packed, the press reported, that 'it would have been possible to walk upon their heads', and the noise was described as quite deafening.

In August 1846 the queen and the prince took a cruise along the south coast of Devon and Cornwall. Although it was an exceptionally wet summer, she was magnanimous enough to write in glowing terms of the enchanting coastline, particularly at Babbacombe and Dartmouth; 'Notwithstanding the rain, this place is lovely, with its wooded rocks and church and castle at the entrance.'

King Edward VII
Albert Edward, Prince of Wales, later King Edward VII, was a frequent visitor to Plymouth. In July 1860 he sailed from Plymouth Sound to Canada and the United States, where he was to undertake a tour lasting four months, returning home via Plymouth again in November.

In November 1865 he and the Princess of Wales anchored on the royal yacht *Osborne* at Barnpool in torrential rain, visited the Royal Agricultural Show at Pennycomequick, and the Tamar Bridge, and attended a ball in the mess at Royal William Yard.

In August 1874 he returned to open the new Guildhall and municipal buildings. The Guildhall's row of stained-glass double windows (destroyed in the blitz in 1941) recorded famous passages in Plymouth's history, the last representing the opening ceremony itself, with the heir to the throne resplendent in frock coat and top hat.

On 18 October 1877 he visited Dartmouth where he personally entered and saw his sons, Princes Albert Victor and George (later King George V) as naval cadets beginning their service on HMS *Britannia*.

On 7 March 1902, five months before their coronation, King Edward VII and Queen Alexandra came to lay the foundation stone for the Dartmouth Royal Naval College, and then to Devonport Dockyard to launch the battleship HMS *Queen*, and to lay the keel-plate of *King Edward VII*, to be launched in 1903.

Victoria, Princess Royal

In August 1887 the Princess Royal, Crown Princess Frederick William of Germany, visited Flete, near Modbury. She was so impressed with the house that when she came to build Friedrichshof, her own home in Germany, after the death of her husband, Emperor Frederick III, she requested the architect to model it particularly on Flete, and sent him to England so he could inspect the property and make notes on its main features.

Alfred, Duke of Edinburgh

Prince Alfred, Queen Victoria's second son, Admiral of the Royal Navy and former Commander-in-Chief of the Mediterranean Fleet, was appointed Commander-in-Chief at Devonport for a period of office lasting almost three years, from August 1890 to June 1893. His official residence while in the town was Admiralty House, later Hamoaze House. During his time there, he was often seen at naval functions and ceremonies, including one of unveiling the Armada memorial on 21 October 1890. An enthusiastic if not necessarily very proficient amateur self-taught violinist (some of the family and household considered his skills somewhat overrated), he joined the Plymouth Orchestral Society, played in concerts at the Guildhall, and secured for Plymouth a visit and two concerts from the Royal Orchestral Society, of which he was President. His appointment came to an end on 3 June 1893, the day he was promoted to Admiral of the Fleet.

King George VI and Queen Elizabeth

Since 1900 there have been many royal visits to Devon, so mention of three of the most important here must suffice. In July 1939 King George VI and Queen Elizabeth and their daughters, Princesses Elizabeth and Margaret, sailing on HM Yacht *Victoria and*

Albert, visited Dartmouth Naval College, where Prince Philip of Greece and Denmark was a naval cadet. The prince accompanied them and his uncle, Lord Louis Mountbatten, dined with them on board, and the following day came back on board with them for tea. Mountbatten noticed that he 'was a great success with children'. Eight years later, in November 1947, Elizabeth, her father's heir to the throne, and Philip were married.

In March 1941 the king and queen came to Plymouth for a tour of the dockyard and an inspection of the civil defence and voluntary services in Guildhall Square. When a warden told the queen that the people of the city were 'keeping their chins up', she replied that 'It is only by keeping our chins up, as we are doing, that we shall win the war.' A little over three hours after they left, an alert was sounded, and a sustained campaign of bombing the city, the blitz, began in earnest. (See p. 150)

On 2 August 1945 King George VI came to Plymouth to greet President Harry Truman of the USA when the latter broke his journey home from Berlin where he had been attending the Potsdam conference at the end of the Second World War. They met aboard HMS *Renown,* moored in Plymouth Sound. Several thousand eager Plymouthians turned out to welcome him, but the route had been changed at the last moment, and even the police were unaware of the exact plan. For a few hours, it appeared that the president was more closely guarded than the king. Only a few selected representatives from the press were allowed within close range of Truman, and there was general disappointment that he saw very little if anything of the blitzed city centre.

WHAT ROYALTY SAID ABOUT DEVON

'We steamed past the various places on the beautiful coast of Devonshire which we had passed three years ago – Seaton, Sidmouth, off which we stopped for ten minutes, Axmouth, Teignmouth, &c.; - till we came to Babbicombe, a small bay, where we remained an hour. It is a beautiful spot, which before we had only passed at a distance. Red cliffs and rocks with wooded hills like Italy, and reminding one of a ballet or play where nymphs are to appear – such rocks and grottos, with the deepest sea, on which there was not a ripple . . . We proceeded on our course again at half past one o'clock, and saw Torquay very plainly, which is very fine. The sea looked so stormy and the weather became so thick that it was thought best to give up Plymouth (for the third time), and to put into that beautiful Dartmouth, and we accordingly did so, in pouring rain, the deck swimming with water, and all of us with umbrellas . . . Notwithstanding the rain, this place is lovely, with its wooded rocks and church and castle at the entrance. It puts me much in mind of the beautiful Rhine, and its fine ruined castles, and the Lurlei.'

Queen Victoria, on board HM Yacht *Victoria and Albert*, Dartmouth, 20 August 1846 (*Leaves from the Life of Our Journal in the Highlands*, etc., 1868)

'At about 4 we approached Plymouth Harbour. It is a magnificent place and the breakwater is wonderful indeed . . . we arrived at Plymouth at 5. It is a beautiful town and we were very well received.'

Princess Victoria of Kent, later queen, in her journal, 2 August 1833 (*The Girlhood of Queen Victoria*, Vol. I, 1912). Earlier in the same paragraph, she recorded that she had been sick for half an hour, but she evidently made a rapid recovery as the next sentence refers to her consumption of a hot mutton chop. The sea air must have been bracing.

'The country is quite lovely and the house very fine, half new and half old, done with great taste and skill and refinement, all beautifully finished . . . The situation of the house is charming. Membland is just as attractive in its way, of course, not nearly so important in size or style, but so comfortable and in such good taste.'

Victoria, Princess Royal, Crown Princess of Prussia, in a letter to Queen Victoria, 28 August 1887, on Membland and the surrounding countryside (*Beloved and Darling Child*, ed. Agatha Ramm, 1990)

'Well here I am in my house which is not ready, & I don't know when it will be, & staying in an hotel by myself, comfortable no doubt as far as hostelries go but more like a commercial traveller than a Commander in Chief.'

Alfred, Duke of Edinburgh, in a letter to Prince Louis of Battenberg, 2 October 1890, from the Devonport Royal Hotel, where he had to stay until Admiralty House was ready for him and his family (*Dearest Affie*, John Van der Kiste, 1984)

'Just got back more dead than alive from a 6 hr tour of visits on the Duchy property which included tenants, farms, tin mine & God knows what!! But I started my sordid day at 6.00 a.m. when I had to step out of the train at Newton Abbot & look happy & pleased with a loyal 'reception'! Gud! [*sic*] But it was some strain sweetheart and the same thing happened at another little town called Ashburton. . . .'

Edward, Prince of Wales, to Freda Dudley Ward, 10 June 1919, from the Duchy Hotel, Princetown (*Letters from a Prince*, ed. Rupert Godfrey, 1998). The Prince of Wales is also Duke of Cornwall, part of which comprises properties on Dartmoor, and the future King Edward VIII was evidently a reluctant visitor.

'Devonport never came up to the enchantment of Malta with its southern sun and mysterious eastern atmosphere; but there was the sea . . . and there was also that beautiful county of Devonshire, so enchanting with its hills and dales, its rivers and forests, its steep roads and high hedges, beautiful gardens and, in places, quite southern vegetation.'

Princess Marie of Edinburgh, later Queen of Roumania, who lived at Admiralty House, Devonport, for several years of her childhood while her father Prince Alfred was Commander-in-Chief (*The Story of my Life*, Vol. I, 1934)

DEVON POLITICIANS & POLITICS

Throughout the nineteenth and early twentieth centuries, Devon sent Conservative and Liberal Unionist (who merged in 1912 to form the Conservative and Unionist Party) and Liberal MPs to Westminster in broadly similar numbers. The county's only Labour MP before 1945, Jimmy Moses, was elected for Plymouth Drake in

1929, defeating the sitting Conservative MP Arthur Shirley Benn by 2,011 votes. A few weeks later a petition was presented alleging bribery and corruption on the part of Moses's agent, but after an eight-day hearing he was cleared of all charges and awarded £3,000 costs. He was defeated at the next election in 1931. In the general election held immediately after the Second World War in 1945, all three Plymouth seats elected Labour MPs. The best-known, Plymouth-born Michael Foot, held Devonport until he was narrowly defeated in 1955, and after trying to regain his seat in 1959 he was subsequently returned at a by-election at Ebbw Vale in 1960. He was leader of the Labour Party from 1980 to 1983.

Foot was the most famous member of a famous Plymouth family. His father Isaac was a former Liberal MP for Bodmin – having unsuccessfully stood in the by-election of November 1919 which sent Lady Astor to Westminster at the start of her career – and co-founder of the local solicitors' firm, Foot & Bowden, in 1903, now Foot Anstey. Of his brothers, Dingle was successively a Liberal and later a Labour MP, outside Devon, while Hugh, later Baron Caradon, was a British ambassador to the United Nations, and John was also a solicitor. Michael was also a prolific journalist and author, his books including biographies of Aneurin Bevan and H.G. Wells, and an honorary member of Plymouth Argyle Football Club, which he had supported since childhood.

Viscount Palmerston, Foreign Secretary and subsequently Prime Minister in the mid-nineteenth century, was one of two MPs for Tiverton, a seat he represented from 1835 until his death in 1865. A few years earlier Spencer Perceval, namesake and son of the only British Prime Minister ever to be assassinated, also sat for the same constituency. Lord John Russell, Palmerston's successor as Prime Minister, and also previously Foreign Secretary, sat for three different constituencies in the county at various times, namely Tavistock from 1813 to 1817, from 1818 to 1820, from 1830 to 1831, then for Devonshire 1831 to 1832, and thereafter for South Devonshire from 1832 to 1835.

For just over two years, after the general election of 1955, every seat in Devon was Conservative-held. This monopoly was broken at a by-election in Torrington in March 1958 when Mark Bonham

Carter (Liberal) won the seat by 219 votes. He was defeated at the subsequent general election in 1959, but this was balanced when the neighbouring seat of North Devon was won by Jeremy Thorpe. He was elected Liberal leader in 1967, resigned in 1976 and was defeated in 1979.

Nancy, Lady Astor, became the first woman MP to sit at Westminster (the first elected woman MP, Countess Markievicz, belonged to Sinn Féin and never took her seat). A by-election was held on 28 November 1919 at Plymouth Sutton following the elevation of the sitting Coalition Unionist member, Waldorf Astor, to the peerage as Viscount Astor after the death of his father and his subsequent resignation from the House of Commons. His wife Nancy stood as candidate in his place and won 14,495 votes, against 9,292 for Mr W.T. Gay (Labour) and 4,139 for Isaac Foot (Liberal), father of Michael, giving her a majority of 5,203 votes, and a majority of 1,064 over the combined vote of both opponents. She represented Sutton as a Coalition Unionist and Conservative until the dissolution of parliament at the end of the Second World War in 1945, when she reluctantly stood down to avoid certain defeat, and the seat was won by another woman, Lucy Middleton (Labour). The latter was defeated in 1951, by Lady Astor's son John Jacob Astor (Conservative), who represented the constituency until 1959.

Leslie Hore-Belisha, born at Devonport, won Plymouth Devonport on his second attempt in 1923 as a Liberal. During the National Government from 1931 onwards, he was a cabinet minister, firstly Minister of Transport (introducing the driving test and giving his name to the Belisha Beacon on pedestrian crossings), and then Minister of War. Defeated in 1945 by Michael Foot, he joined the Conservatives and was made a peer in 1954.

Dr David Owen, born at Plympton, won Plymouth Sutton in 1966 for the Labour party, and was then elected for Plymouth Devonport in 1974 after the boundaries were redrawn, joining the cabinet as Foreign Secretary in 1977. In 1981 he was one of the 'Gang of Four' who formed the Social Democratic Party, and after becoming party leader continued to sit in Parliament until 1992 when he stood down and went to the House of Lords as Baron Owen of the City of Plymouth.

Alan 'Howling Laud' Hope (1942–), leader of the Official Monster Raving Loony Party (OMRLP) since 1999, was formerly landlord of the Golden Lion public house, Ashburton, which was the party's headquarters and conference centre from 1984 to 2000, when he sold it and moved to Hampshire. He was elected unopposed to a seat on Ashburton Town Council in 1987 under the party colours, but at the time, under party rules any member who won an election to public office was automatically expelled, so at the next conference the rule had to be altered. He later became deputy mayor, and in 1998 mayor. From 1999 he and his ginger tabby, Cat Mandu, were joint party leaders, until the latter's death in a road accident in 2002.

Roger Knapman, who was born and lives in Devon, was leader of the United Kingdom Independence Party (UKIP) from 2002 to 2006. A Conservative MP for Stroud in Gloucestershire from 1987 to 1997, he contested Devon North in the 2001 general election and Totnes in 2005, coming fourth on both occasions.

Between 1951 and 1955, Devon sent no women to Westminster. In the latter year, Joan Vickers (Conservative) won Plymouth Devonport from Michael Foot with a 100-vote majority. Women subsequently elected include Gwyneth Dunwoody (Labour), Exeter 1966–70; Janet Fookes (Conservative), Plymouth Drake 1974–92; Emma Nicholson (Conservative, later Liberal Democrat), Torridge and West Devon 1987–97; Angela Browning (Conservative), Tiverton 1992–97, Tiverton and Honiton 1997–2010; and Linda Gilroy (Labour), Plymouth Sutton 1997–2010. In 2010 three women were elected, namely Alison Seabeck (Labour), Plymouth Moor View (she had sat for Plymouth Devonport since 2005); Anne Marie Morris (Conservative), Newton Abbot; and Dr Sarah Wollaston (Conservative), Totnes.

Devon's smallest majority was in December 1910 when the Liberal candidate at Exeter, H. St Maur, defeated his Unionist opponent, H.E. Duke, by four votes. As the result of an election petition and scrutiny of the ballot papers, four months later Mr Duke was declared elected by one vote. In 1923 Francis Acland (Liberal), narrowly triumphed over his cousin, Lt-Col F.D. Acland-Troyte (Unionist), with a majority of three votes. The latter won the seat in at the subsequent general election in 1924 and held it comfortably until he retired in 1945.

The most nail-biting result in recent years was at the 1997 general election, when Rupert Allason, Conservative MP for Torbay, saw his 5,787 majority overturned by Adrian Sanders for the Liberal Democrats with a majority of 12.

LADY ASTOR SAID . . .

The Rt Hon Member for Plymouth Sutton was legendary for her repartee, and the following quotations have been attributed to her, though sometimes to others instead:

'One reason why I don't drink is because I wish to know when I am having a good time.'

'My vigour, vitality, and cheek repel me. I am the kind of woman I would run from.'

'Women have got to make the world safe for men since men have made it so darned unsafe for women.'

'We women talk too much, but even then we don't tell half what we know.'

'I married beneath me. All women do.'

'The only thing I like about rich people is their money.'

'No one sex can govern alone. I believe that one of the reasons why civilisation has failed so lamentably is that it has had one-sided government.'

'Is it my birthday or am I dying?' – to her family, seeing them gathered around her bedside during her last illness. One allegedly replied, 'A bit of both, Mama.'

'Why don't you come sober, Prime Minister?' – to Winston Churchill, when he asked her what disguise he ought to wear to a masked ball.

'If you were my husband, I'd poison your tea' – again, to Churchill, who replied, 'Madam, if you were my wife, I'd drink it.'

'You're not handsome enough to have such fears' – yet again to Churchill, when he said that having a woman in parliament was like having one intrude on him while he was in the bath.

DEVON'S IRISH NATIONALIST CONNECTION

Anna Parnell, a prominent Irish political activist and journalist, and younger sister of the Nationalist leader Charles Stewart Parnell, withdrew from public life after falling out with her brother, left Ireland and came to live in Devon. Although she wrote occasional letters to the press, she spent most of her time painting and writing poetry under the name Cerisa Palmer, keen not to court publicity. She was lodging at Avenue Road, Ilfracombe, when she went swimming at the beach on 20 September 1911 and drowned, aged fifty-nine. Her body was laid to rest at Holy Trinity Church.

2

ARTISTS, ARCHITECTS, MUSICIANS & ACTORS

DEVON PAINTERS

Nicholas Hilliard (1547–1619), son of an Exeter goldsmith, was himself a goldsmith, carver and limner to Queen Elizabeth, and is regarded as England's first major painter of miniatures.

Thomas Hudson (1701–79), was an Exeter-born portrait painter and one of the most famous of his day, his sitters including King George II, the Duke of Marlborough, and Handel.

Sir Joshua Reynolds (1723–92), born at Plympton St Maurice, was the son of the local schoolmaster. He set himself up as a portrait painter at Devonport, but later moved to London where he became the most fashionable portrait painter of his day, and was elected the first President of the Royal Academy of Arts when it was founded in 1768. A friend of the Earl of Morley and his family at Saltram, he was a frequent visitor there, and several of his portraits of the family can still be seen at the house.

Richard Cosway (1740–1821) was a Tiverton-born painter of portraits and miniatures, from whom King George IV commissioned several works.

James Northcote (1746–1831) was a Plymouth-born painter of historical pictures and portraits, who like Reynolds had to move to London to find success. His best-known painting, 'A Scene from Shakespeare's Richard II', is in Exeter Art Gallery.

Samuel Prout (1783–1852) was a Plymouth-born watercolour landscape and townscape painter, who became Painter in Watercolours in Ordinary to King George IV, King William IV, and Queen Victoria.

Benjamin Robert Haydon (1786–1846), writer on art and painter of historical scenes, rarely achieved the success he strove for, and his debt-ridden life ended in suicide.

Sir Charles Eastlake (1793–1865) was a painter of historical pictures, including one of Napoleon Bonaparte on board *Bellerophon* in Plymouth Sound, and later successively the first Keeper and Director of the National Gallery, and President of the Royal Academy.

Frederick John Widgery (1861–1942), an Exeter city councillor and mayor from 1903 to 1904, was one of the most prolific Dartmoor painters, mostly dealing in watercolour but occasionally in oils. He is one of several names from the nineteenth and twentieth centuries who has always been revered (and collected) in his own county but almost completely unknown outside it. Others include his father William Widgery (1826–93); Charles E. Brittan Senior (1837–88); his son, Charles E. Brittan Junior (1870–1949); George Henry Jenkins (1843–1914), Daniel Sherrin (1868–1940) and – you guessed it – his son, Reginald Daniel Sherrin (1891–1971).

Beryl Cook (1926–2008), a self-taught artist who ran a guest house in Plymouth, initially painted colourful pictures of everyday life in Plymouth, often featuring jolly plump (in other words, plump and jolly) women, and whose bold style made her one of the best-loved artists of her day.

Robert Lenkiewicz (1941–2002), was a controversial artist based in studio at the Barbican, Plymouth, whose portraits of people focused on themes such as death, vagrancy and social handicap (see p. 176).

George Passmore (1942–), of the collaborative duo of artists Gilbert and George, was born in Plymouth.

PAINTERS WHO VISITED DEVON

Richard Wilson (1714–82) visited the county in 1771, and painted studies of Okehampton Castle and Lydford.

Joseph Mallord William Turner (1775–1851) was London born and bred, though his father came from South Molton. He paid at least three visits to various parts of Devon, and painted several landscapes of the county, especially around the Plymouth area and on Dartmoor. His major watercolour, 'Plymouth from Mount Edgcumbe' was acquired by Plymouth City Museum and Art Gallery in 2006.

Thomas Girtin (1775–1802), regarded as the founder of modern watercolour painting, visited South Devon in 1800 and painted several pictures, the best-known being 'Rainbow over the Exe'.

Samuel Palmer (1805–81), one of the major Romantic painters, lived mainly in London and Surrey, but visited North Devon at least twice during his lifetime, where he painted pictures of Lee Abbey and Ilfracombe.

John William Inchbold (1830–88), a landscape painter strongly associated with the Pre-Raphaelites, was born and died in Leeds but travelled extensively. His earliest paintings, from the 1850s, include 'The Moorland (Dewar-Stone)' and 'Devonshire Coast', both in Tate Britain, and 'Anstey's Cove', in the Fitzwilliam Museum, Cambridge.

DEVON ARCHITECTS

Nicholas Stone (1586–1647) built several tombs and sepulchral monuments, although no examples of his work have been identified in his native county.

John Foulston (1772–1841) was from London, but his major work was done in Devon. His best-known creations were the Greek Doric town hall and commemorative column in Ker Street, Devonport, and he was also responsible for the creation of Union Street, built across marshland to link (or unite) the three towns of Plymouth, Devonport and Stonehouse, hence the name. He also designed and built the original Theatre Royal and Assembly Rooms, the Royal Union Baths and St Catherine's Church, Plymouth, and a terrace of houses in Roman Corinthian style in Devonport, all long since demolished to make way for newer buildings or destroyed in the Second World War. He also built a ballroom in Torquay, and restored the medieval abbey gatehouse at Tavistock in Gothic style.

Charles Fowler (1800–67) built the lower and higher markets in Exeter during the 1830s, as well as a few churches in Devon, notably St Paul's, Honiton.

Sir George Gilbert Scott (1811–78), although not a Devon man, was among the most prolific of British architects involved with the design, building and refurbishment of many churches, cathedrals and workhouses in England, and it is estimated that he designed or renovated over 800 buildings altogether. Among those in Devon with which he was involved are the workhouses at Totnes, Bideford, Newton Abbot and Tavistock, all in the 1830s, and the restoration of Exeter Cathedral, of St Mary's Church and the Priory Church, both at Totnes, about thirty years later.

Sir William White (1845–1913) was a Devonport-born naval architect, warship designer, Director of Naval Construction at the Admiralty and Assistant Controller of the Navy, who during his career bore ultimate responsibility for the design of 33 battleships, 26 armoured cruisers and 102 protected cruisers. He is not to be confused with contemporary architect William White (1825–1900), who was not a local man but well-known for his role in nineteenth-century Gothic Revival architecture and restored many Devon churches, including those of Holy Trinity Church, Barnstaple; Church of John the Baptist, Instow; and Bishop's Court, the former Bishop's Palace, Sowton.

George Prynne (1853–1927) helped to restore, rebuild and design several churches in England, including the new organ case and pulpit at St Andrew's Church, Ashburton, and the wooden screen at St Peter's Church, Buckland-in-the-Moor.

DEVON MUSICIANS & COMPOSERS

Robert Stone (*c.* 1516–1613), composer and member of the Chapel Royal, is best known for his setting of the Lord's Prayer, completed in about 1550.

Matthew Locke (*c.* 1630–77), born at Exeter, composed the music for the processional march for the coronation of Charles II.

William Jackson (1730–1803) was for many years the organist at Exeter Cathedral, the city where he was born and died. He wrote and published several sonatas, secular and sacred vocal works, and an opera, though none of these are particularly well remembered today. He was one of the most versatile men of his time, being also a writer and publisher of essays, and a landscape painter who exhibited at the Royal Academy.

Henry Francis Lyte (1793–1847), Anglican divine and hymn writer, lived successively at Dittisham, Charleton and Brixham. It was at the latter that he wrote his most famous hymns, including three paraphrases of the Psalms, notably 'Praise my soul, the King of Heaven' (Psalm 103), and after taking his last service, 'Abide

with me', said to have been inspired partly by watching the sun setting over Torbay.

Samuel Sebastian Wesley (1810–76), a grandson of Charles Wesley, like Jackson, was born at Exeter and was cathedral organist. His works include 'The European Psalmist', and 'Twelve Anthems and Responses'.

Elias Parish-Alvars (1810–49), Teignmouth-born composer and harpist, wrote more than eighty compositions for the instrument, including two concertos, and duos for harp and piano.

Franz Liszt (1811–86) gave a series of piano recitals in England in August 1840, including one at the Royal Clarence Hotel, Exeter, and another at the Manor Hotel, Exmouth.

Sir W.S. Gilbert (1836–1911) and Sir Arthur Sullivan (1842–1900), librettist and composer respectively of the Savoy Operas, staged the first performance of their operetta *The Pirates of Penzance* at the Bijou Theatre, Paignton, on 31 December 1878. It was given by a D'Oyly Carte touring company who were in Devon at the time, playing *HMS Pinafore* in Torquay during the evening. The Paignton show was a one-off, solely to enable the writers to establish their copyright in the work, with the cast reading and singing from scripts carried on stage, making do with any costumes available.

A second county link with Gilbert and Sullivan is to be found at Coleton Fishacre, an Art Deco house near Kingswear built as a holiday home for the D'Oyly Carte family in the 1920s. They subsequently sold it and it is now a National Trust property, furnished partly as a museum with exhibits pertaining to the family and the famous duo.

Percy Whitlock (1903–46), Borough Organist at the Bournemouth Municipal Pavilion, and music director at St Stephen's Church, Bournemouth, composed *Plymouth Suite,* which was begun before and completed after he and his wife Edna had attended an Incorporated Association of Organists Congress at Plymouth in August and September 1939. The closing movement, *Toccata*, was dedicated to Dr Harold George Moreton, Plymouth Borough Organist, 'a sprightly fellow who has been shabbily treated by the corporation, who are mercenary.'

Ron Goodwin (1925–2003), Plymouth-born composer, arranger, orchestrator and conductor, was commissioned by Plymouth City Fathers to write the *Drake 400 Suite*, given its first performance in 1980 to mark the celebrations for the Tudor explorer's epic journey around the world, and the *Armada 400 Suite* for similar festivities eight years later.

POP, ROCK & JAZZ TRIVIA

Glenn Miller and his Band played what would be one of their last concerts in Plymouth, at the Odeon, on 28 August 1944. He then left for Europe in order to plan a six-week tour, boarding a flight for Paris on 15 December to supervise arrangements in advance. The plane went missing over the English Channel.

The Beatles played concerts at Exeter three times, and Plymouth twice, on each occasion at the respective cities' ABC venue. The Exeter dates were 28 March 1963, supporting American singers Tommy Roe and Chris Montez (the only one of the five dates they were not topping the bill), 14 November 1963 and 28 October 1964. The Plymouth dates were 13 November 1963 and 29 October 1964. They also made an unscheduled appearance in Devon in September 1967 while filming the movie *Magical Mystery Tour*. Plans to visit Widecombe Fair and shoot some of the footage there were cancelled when their bus became wedged on a narrow bridge on Dartmoor (one had no sat navs to blame in those days), and John Lennon lost his temper. So they turned round, leaving the road crew to sort the problem out, and went for a day in Plymouth, where they had lunch at the Grand Hoe Hotel, and sat on the Hoe overlooking the Sound. Unlike on the previous West Country visits, although they were among the four most recognisable people in Britain, they had no qualms about being seen in public, and no fear of being mobbed by hysterical fans.

The Rolling Stones played dates at Exeter three times; the ABC on 26 August 1964 (followed by the Plymouth ABC the following evening), and the Odeon on 2 October 1964 and 16 July 1965. On the latter they shared the bill with the Walker Brothers and the then little-known Rod Stewart. Drummer Charlie Watts has for some years owned an Arabian horse stud farm at Dolton, while Bill Wyman's Rhythm Kings, the band their former bass guitarist formed in 1997, have played gigs at venues in Plymouth and Barnstaple.

The Silkie were a folk quartet who formed after meeting at Hull University, although guitarist Mike Ramsden was from Totnes. Their only success was with a Top 30 version of the Beatles' 'You've Got To Hide Your Love Away' in 1965. They disbanded the following year. Ramsden and vocalist Sylvia Tatler married and settled in Devon, keeping the name alive, sometimes as a duo, sometimes with their children, and often performed at their local, the Cott Inn, Dartington, until shortly before Ramsden's death in 2004.

The Rustics, from Paignton, won a Westward TV beat contest in 1964 and were signed up by Beatles manager Brian Epstein, though they failed to emulate the success of the Liverpool acts he had already signed and turned into household names. Three of the group, and Ramsden from The Silkie, were together at King Edward VI Grammar School, Totnes.

Paul Simon was for years believed to have been inspired by the medieval bridge at Bickleigh over the Exe when writing 'Bridge Over Troubled Water', released in 1970. Although he is known to have stayed in the village in the mid-1960s, his musical partner Art Garfunkel quashed the rumour in an interview on BBC Radio Devon with local presenter Judi Spiers in 2003, stating that Simon had taken the phrase from an old Baptist hymn. Shortly before he became a household name, Simon had spent some time playing low-key concerts, mainly in folk clubs, throughout Britain, including one at Newhayes House, Exeter, in 1965.

Emerson, Lake & Palmer played their first ever live show at Plymouth Guildhall, to a capacity crowd of 3,000, featuring the material they would be performing at the Isle of Wight Festival the following week. Featuring Keith Emerson (piano, organ, custom Moog and Hammond organ), Greg Lake (bass) and Carl Palmer (drums), they played a set including 'Rondo' and 'America', both of which had been part of Emerson's repertoire during his leadership of previous band The Nice, and their arrangement of Mussorgsky's suite 'Pictures at an Exhibition'.

McGuinness Flint needed a picturesque backdrop to the photoshoot for the sleeve of their eponymous debut album in 1970, so their manager decided to dress them up as Victorian gravediggers and pose them against the Church of St Michael, Brentor. They travelled there overnight from London in a van, and arrived on a wet autumn morning to find the church surrounded with scaffolding. As nobody fancied returning home, waiting for repairs to be finished, and making the journey to Devon again another day when the church was once again in its more natural state, a certain amount of airbrushing on the final photos was therefore required.

Fairport Convention wrote, recorded and released 'Babbacombe Lee', often hailed as the world's first folk rock opera, in 1971. Based on the story of John Lee, 'the man they couldn't hang' (see p. 65), the group's fiddle player Dave Swarbrick was inspired to write it after he discovered a file of old newspaper clippings in a junk shop, containing Lee's own copies of the articles, bound by him, signed and dated 30 January 1908.

Sparks, at the time a five-piece group consisting of American brothers Ron and Russell Mael plus three British musicians, played at Home Park, Plymouth, on 2 July 1974. They stayed at the Holiday Inn, and settled a bill for £400, a sum claimed as inadequate by management for the damage they and their entourage had caused, citing a broken lift and colour TV, and costs for cleaning a bedroom carpet – quite apart from their disturbing other guests with a rowdy party at 3 a.m. and attacking staff with water pistols. Their manager John Hewlett denied the alleged incidents and unruly behaviour, and claimed the only damage they admitted was when they dropped minestrone soup on a carpet, not vomit as the management had claimed. As for 'attacks' on hotel staff, he said water pistols were 'part of the fun of life'.

Yes originally planned to call their 1978 album *Yes Tor*, after the rock formation on Dartmoor. It was renamed *Tormato* prior to release, but a photograph of Yes Tor was still used on the front cover.

Ian Hunter, lead singer of Mott The Hoople until leaving them in 1974, made his debut as a solo artist with his new band at Exeter University on 18 March 1975, where he played a warm-up gig prior to a short British tour.

Cozy Powell, the drummer, named one track on *Octopuss*, his 1983 solo album, 'Dartmoore', although this was thought to owe more to its writer, guitarist Gary Moore, than to any inspiration from the area itself.

Show of Hands, a folk, acoustic and roots duo comprising Steve Knightley and Phil Beer, were formed in Devon in 1991. Both had met as teenagers while playing in different bands in Exeter. After working with others over the years, they played together casually during the 1980s, until deciding to unite full time early the following decade.

Seth Lakeman, folk singer-songwriter and multi-instrumentalist, was born at Buckland Monachorum in 1977. His first three albums, *The Punch Bowl* (2002), *Kitty Jay* (2004), nominated for the Mercury Music Prize, and *Freedom Fields* (2006), all recorded in Devon, were partly inspired by local historical themes.

Muse were formed in 1994 by students at Teignmouth Community College. When they returned to the town to play two gigs at The Den on 4 and 5 September 2007 to celebrate the release of their fifth album *The Resistance*, according to a national paper, 'streets were cordoned off, barricades erected and the entire population seemed to have turned out to celebrate the returning heroes.'

Michael Jackson paid an unscheduled visit to Exeter City Football Club in June 2002 with his friend Uri Geller, and was made an honorary director. He admitted he knew nothing about football but he 'loved' Exeter City, and was now entitled to play a full part in the club's boardroom, including voting on key decisions about players, free admission to any games he might want to attend, and to travel to away matches with players on the club coach. As far as is known, during the remaining seven years of his life he never used any of these privileges, let alone played any benefit gigs at Exeter.

Jimmy Page of Led Zeppelin, a keen admirer and collector of the work of Victorian architect and furniture designer William Burges, loaned a wardrobe to and opened an exhibition of Burges at Knightshayes Court, near Tiverton, in May 2002.

Joss Stone, born Jocelyn Stoker, moved to Devon as a child and spent her teenage years living in Ashill, near Cullompton, and went to school at Uffculme.

POP & ROCK STARS BORN IN DEVON

Tony Burrows, singer with various groups, mainly on record only,
    including the Kestrels, Ivy League, Flowerpot Men, Edison
    Lighthouse, White Plains, Brotherhood of Man, Pipkins, and
    First Class – Exeter, 1942
Peter Quaife, bass guitarist, the Kinks – Tavistock, 1943 (died 2010)
Dave Hill, guitarist, Slade – Flete, near Modbury, 1946
Martin Turner, singer and bass guitarist, Wishbone Ash –
    Torquay, 1947
John Gosling, keyboards player, the Kinks – Paignton, 1948
Snowy White, guitarist, Thin Lizzy – Barnstaple, 1948
Julian Marshall, keyboards, Marshall Hain, Flying Lizards –
    Exeter, 1954
Beth Gibbons, vocalist, Portishead – Exeter, 1965
Chris Martin, singer and guitarist, Coldplay – Exeter, 1977
Jim Causley, singer-songwriter – Exeter, 1980
Sergio Pizzorno, guitarist, Kasabian – Newton Abbot, 1980
Rebecca Worthley, singer-songwriter – Exeter, 1981
Jon Lee, vocalist, S Club 7 – Ipplepen, 1982

MUSIC VENUES

Most licensed premises stage live concerts and gigs at one time
or another, as do universities and colleges, and this short list only
comprises the major venues.

> Barnfield Music Club, Exeter
> Guildhall, Plymouth
> Home Park, Plymouth
> Matchroom Cabaret, Plymouth
> Pavilions, Plymouth
> Riviera International Centre, Torquay
> Spinning Wheel, Paignton
> Westpoint Arena, Clyst St Mary, Exeter
> White Rabbit, Plymouth

Home Park is not immediately thought of as a music venue, but
in recent years has been host to concerts from megastars including

Rod Stewart, Elton John and George Michael. The Plymouth Guildhall now only stages classical concerts, but in the 1970s hosted gigs from the top rock and pop acts of the time, including Slade, Status Quo, Electric Light Orchestra, Wizzard, Lindisfarne, Mud and the Bay City Rollers.

Many other music venues have been and gone; and the following all staged major concerts and shows by major names.

> ABC, Plymouth and Exeter
> Queens Hall, Barnstaple (now Queens Hall Theatre)
> Van Dike Club, Plymouth
> Woods, Plymouth

The ABC was the only venue to host shows by the Beatles and the Rolling Stones (see p. 28).

ACTORS, PERFORMERS, BROADCASTERS & IMPRESARIOS

Cora Pearl (*c*. 1835– 86), born Emma Crouch, claimed to have been born in Caroline Place, East Stonehouse, Plymouth, in 1842, though she was more probably born in London seven years earlier and moved to Plymouth in infancy. She was one of the most notorious courtesans in England and France of her time, but a brief theatrical career only served to emphasise her severely limited talents.

Fred Karno (1866–1941) real name Frederick Westcott, born at Exeter, was one of the leading music hall impresarios. He is credited as inventor of the custard pie in face gag, as well as the man who nurtured the careers of Charlie Chaplin and Stan Laurel. His career did not survive the advent of the cinema and he went bankrupt in 1925.

Stan Laurel (1890–1965) and Oliver Hardy (1892–1957) played what turned out to be the final show of their career at the Palace Theatre, Plymouth, on 17 May 1954. Their *Birds of a Feather* was the star turn of a variety bill which was due to play all week, but after one performance Hardy, already fighting a viral infection, was confined to bed at the Grand Hotel after a mild heart attack. Laurel withdrew from the bill as well, which went ahead with only the support acts.

Rachel Kempson (1910–2003), born in Dartmouth, and later wife of Sir Michael Redgrave, was a star of stage and screen, including several performances with the Royal Shakespeare Company, and roles in films including *Tom Jones* (1963), *Out of Africa* (1985), as well as BBC TV's *The Jewel in the Crown* (1984).

Sir Donald Sinden (1923–), born in Plymouth and also subsequently an RSC member, similarly enjoyed a long career in the theatre, films and TV, including films *The Cruel Sea* (1953), *Above Us the Waves* (1955), and on TV the situation comedy *Never the Twain* (1981–91) and the drama *Judge John Deed* (2001–7).

Peter Cook (1937–95) born in Torquay, was one of the most renowned satirists and comedians of his day. He married his third wife Chiew Lin Chong in Torbay in 1989.

Ed Stewart (1941–), born Edward Mainwaring near Exmouth, is a former pirate radio disc jockey turned presenter on BBC radio and TV and independent radio, most associated with BBC Radio 1's *Junior Choice*.

Angela Rippon (1944–), born in Plymouth, was TV's first regular female newsreader and subsequently presenter of various series including *Top Gear* and *Cash in the Attic*, although her most famous role was arguably as a dancer on the *Morecambe and Wise Christmas Special* in 1976.

Actor Charles Dance (1946–) and comedy actress Dawn French (1957–), both born outside Devon, were partly raised and educated in the county. Meanwhile, broadcaster and media executive Noel Edmonds (1948–) has lived in Devon for several years, where he has campaigned and spoken out on environmental issues.

THEATRES

Several theatres have opened and closed in the county's major towns and cities. The following are still active:

Barnstaple, Queen's Theatre
Dartmouth, Flavel Arts Centre
Exeter, Barnfield Theatre
Exeter, Northcott Theatre
Ilfracombe, Landmark Theatre
Paignton, Palace Theatre
Plymouth, Theatre Royal
Teignmouth, Carlton Theatre
Tiverton, New Hall
Torquay, Babbacombe Theatre
Torquay, Princess Theatre
Totnes, Great Hall and Barn Theatre, Dartington Hall

EXETER'S UNFORTUNATE THEATRE HISTORY

During the nineteenth century, the words theatre, fire and Exeter sadly went together all too often. The New Theatre, built in 1787, was destroyed in 1820 when the rafters caught fire from a gas-lit chandelier. The Theatre Royal, built in 1821 to replace it, lasted until 1885, when it was gutted in a similar accident, the sole fatality being a pig that belonged to a clown.

Much more appalling was the tragedy of the new Theatre Royal on 5 September 1887, when some drapes caught fire from a naked gas flame during a performance attended by an audience of about 800. Within a few minutes panic had broken out among patrons

who were desperate to escape. Many were killed not just by the fumes but also from being suffocated in the rush, particularly those who could not get out from the upper floor gallery. Casualty figures vary, but the number for those who died has been put as high as 186. To this date, it remains the highest figure for deaths in a single building incident in Britain. After the subsequent enquiry, stringent safety regulations were made mandatory in the construction of buildings licensed for public entertainment.

FILMS

The following feature films were shot partly on location in Devon.

A Matter of Life and Death (1946), directed by Michael Powell, Emeric Pressburger, starring David Niven, Kim Hunter – Saunton Sands.

Knights of the Round Table (1953), Richard Thorpe, starring Robert Taylor, Kim Gardner – Haytor Vale, Dartmoor.

The System (1964), Michael Winner, starring Oliver Reed, Jane Merrow – Brixham.

Catch Us If You Can (1965), John Boorman, starring The Dave Clark Five, Barbara Ferris – Burgh Island.

Isadora (1968), Karel Reisz, starring Vanessa Redgrave, John Fraser – Oldway Mansion.

Barry Lyndon (1975), Stanley Kubrick, starring Ryan O'Neal, Marisa Berenson, Patrick Magee – Compton Castle.

That Summer (1979), Harley Cokeliss, starring Ray Winstone, Tony London – Torbay.

The French Lieutenant's Woman (1982), Karel Reisz, starring Meryl Streep, Jeremy Irons – Kingswear.

Revolution (1985), Hugh Hudson, starring Al Pacino, Donald Sutherland – Challaborough Bay; Dartmoor.

Ordeal by Innocence (1985), Desmond Davis, starring Donald Sutherland, Faye Dunaway, Christopher Plummer – Dartmouth.

Howards End (1992), James Ivory, starring Emma Thompson, Vanessa Redgrave, Anthony Hopkins – Blackpool Sands.

The Remains of the Day (1993), James Ivory, starring Anthony Hopkins, Emma Thompson, James Fox – Powderham Castle.

Sense and Sensibility (1995), Ang Lee, starring Emma Thompson, Kate Winslet, Alan Rickman – Saltram; Flete.

Churchill: The Hollywood Years (2004), Peter Richardson, starring Jon Culshaw, Tom Clarke Hill, Hamish McColl – Brixham.

TELEVISION

In 1970 the *Monty Python's Flying Circus* team were filming on location in Torbay, and stayed at the Gleneagles Hotel, Torquay, run by Donald Sinclair, a retired naval commander, and his wife. The experience inspired John Cleese to create the BBC situation comedy *Fawlty Towers*, shown in two series in 1975 and 1979, in which Basil Fawlty, played by Cleese, was based largely on Sinclair, whom the actor said was 'the most wonderfully rude man I have ever met.' He alleged that while they were there, Sinclair threw a suitcase belonging to another guest over a cliff as it was ticking and he thought it was a bomb (it contained an alarm clock), and flung a timetable at a guest who asked when the next bus left. Sinclair's widow Beatrice later said that Basil Fawlty was a merciless caricature of her husband who had been 'turned into a laughing stock', the Python team 'behaved so badly it defied belief' while they were on the premises, and Cleese was 'an utter fool' who had 'made millions out of our unhappiness'. Although the programme was set in Torquay, all filming took place in the home counties.

Oldway Mansion, Paignton, has often been used for filming on location as its setting makes it ideal for scenes whenever the set for a stately home is required. TV drama series which have made use of this facility include *Edward the Seventh*, starring Timothy West (ATV, first shown 1975), and *Nancy Astor*, starring Lisa Harrow (BBC, 1982).

The comedy series *Jam and Jerusalem*, starring Sue Johnston, Dawn French, Joanna Lumley and Jennifer Saunders (BBC, 2006–9), set in the fictional West Country town of Clatterford St Mary, was filmed partly in North Tawton and on Dartmoor.

3

LITERATURE & LEARNING

DEVON AUTHORS, BY BIRTH & ASSOCIATION

John Ford (1586–*c*. 1640), born at Ilsington, author of several plays including *'Tis Pity She's a Whore*, is regarded as the only significant tragedian of the early Stuart era.

Robert Herrick (1591–1674) was a poet and vicar of Dean Prior from 1629 until 1646 (when removed by Oliver Cromwell) and again from 1660 until his death. London-born, he had a love-hate relationship with his adopted county. One poem suggested a degree of contentment with rural life which he would never have found in London, another referred to 'loathed Devonshire', and another still to Devonians as 'as rude almost as rudest savages'. At the same time, he described with affection the local flora and fauna, some of the local scenes, and country customs of the county.

John Gay (1685–1732), born in Barnstaple, was a poet and dramatist best remembered for writing *The Beggar's Opera*, said to have 'made Rich [John Rich, his producer] gay, and Gay rich'.

Hannah Cowley (1743–1809), born at Tiverton, was the most successful woman playwright of her time, though little remembered today. She was the author of dramas including *The Belle's Stratagem* and *A School for Greybeards*.

O. Jones, a journeyman woolcomber, is remembered as the author of *Poetic Attempts* (1786), and often referred to as 'the

Devonshire poet', though little if anything else appears to be known about him.

Samuel Taylor Coleridge (1772–1834), born at Ottery St Mary, leading poet of the Romantic era, best remembered for *The Rime of the Ancient Mariner*. In 1797, he and William Wordsworth (1770–1850) visited the Valley of the Rocks, Lynton, together and decided to write a prose tale, *The Wanderings of Cain*, but it was never completed.

Jane Austen (1775–1817) spent a holiday in Devon, and set her first novel, *Sense and Sensibility* (1811), in the village of Upton Pyne, 4 miles from Exeter. The marriage of Elinor Dashwood and Edward Ferrars was set in the village church. Dawlish is also mentioned in the novel.

Charles Dickens (1812–70) wrote the opening chapters of *Nicholas Nickleby* at Mile End Cottage, Alphington, where his parents lived from 1839 to 1843. The Fat Boy in *Pickwick Papers* was based on an overweight boot-boy he saw in the Turk's Head, a fifteenth-century pub in Exeter, which he called 'the most beautiful in this most beautiful of English counties.' Pecksniff, in *Martin Chuzzlewit*, was based on a resident in Topsham. His Christmas short story *A Message From The Sea* opens with a description of Clovelly by one of the central characters, Captain Jorgan – 'And a mighty sing'lar and pretty place it is, as ever I saw in all the days of my life.'

Charles Kingsley (1819–75) was born at Holne where his father was curate. His most popular novel, *Westward Ho!*, was as the title suggests based around North Devon.

Edward Capern (1819–94), 'the postman poet of Bideford', was born at Tiverton and spent most of his life in Devon. He was the author of a patriotic verse, 'The Lion Flag of England', which was published as a broadsheet and sent to troops fighting in the Crimea. The Prime Minister Lord Palmerston was so impressed with it that he sent for Capern and awarded him an annual pension of £60 from the Civil List.

R.D. Blackmore (1825–1900), educated at Blundell's School, Tiverton (see p. 55), spent much of his life in Devon, the scenery of which inspired his novels *Lorna Doone* (Exmoor), and the lesser-known *Christowell* (Dartmoor).

Sir Arthur Conan Doyle (1859–1930) briefly practised as a doctor at Durnford Street, Plymouth – not very successfully, it appears – before deciding to follow his vocation as a writer. His most famous Sherlock Holmes novel, *The Hound of the Baskervilles*, was set on Dartmoor and partly written while he was staying at the Duchy Hotel, Princetown, in 1901.

Eden Phillpotts (1862–1960), a prolific novelist, writer of short stories, poems and plays, lived firstly at Torquay and then at Broadclyst. Eighteen novels and two collections of short stories comprise his Dartmoor cycle, each one of the series taking a specific area of the moor and describing it faithfully.

John Galsworthy (1867–1933) was born at Kingston-upon-Thames, of Devon ancestry. During an affair with his cousin's wife Ada, whom he married after her divorce, they moved to Wingstone Manor, Manaton, on Dartmoor. Unlike Ada, who missed the life of London, he preferred the solitude of Manaton, although she persuaded him to return to the city, where they settled until his death. His short story *The Apple Tree*, on which the film *Summer Story* was based, was set partly in Devon and inspired by the story of Dartmoor girl Kitty Jay, while another tale, *A Man of Devon*, was set in the Torquay and Kingswear areas.

Radclyffe Hall (1880–1943), author of *The Well of Lonliness*, lived briefly at Lynton during the early years of the Second World War.

Agatha Christie (1890–1976), born at Torquay, 'the queen of crime', creator of detectives Hercule Poirot and Miss Marple, and author of the west end's longest-running play *The Mousetrap*, was at one time reportedly the world's best-selling author of thrillers. Some of her books feature references to local landmarks and areas of Devon, including Burgh Island, the cliffs at St Marychurch, the Imperial Hotel, Torquay, and Haytor.

Jean Rhys, born Ella Gwendolen Rees Williams (1890–1979), novelist and short story writer best known for *Wide Sargasso Sea*, spent part of her adult life in Devon. In 1939 she and her second husband Leslie Tilden-Smith settled there for some years. After moving away from the county she returned with her third husband Max Hamer. They lived in Cheriton Fitzpaine, where she was accused on more than one occasion of being a witch. After attacking her accuser with a pair of scissors, she was placed in a mental hospital for a few days. Some years later she died in Exeter Hospital.

L.A.G. Strong (1896–1958) wrote novels, short stories, poems, plays, books for children and non-fiction, as well as broadcasting and lecturing on drama and voice production. He is best remembered for *Dewer Rides*, a novel set on Dartmoor.

Henry Williamson (1897–1977) spent part of his life in North Devon, his experience of the countryside inspiring his most famous novel *Tarka the Otter*.

R.F. Delderfield (1912–72), novelist and playwright, was best remembered for *A Horseman Riding By* and *To Serve Them All My Days*. His brother Eric (d. 1996) was a noted writer of non-fiction, including titles on Devon historic houses and other aspects of local history, inn signs, and kings and queens.

Victor Canning (1916–86) was born in Plymouth, and though the family moved to Oxford in 1925, he always thought of himself as Devonian, and in later life lived at South Molton for a while. A prolific writer of mostly thrillers, he published 61 books and at least 80 short stories.

Alan Clark (1928–99), Conservative MP for Plymouth Sutton, published several books on military history before beginning his political career.

Ted Hughes (1930–98), Poet Laureate from 1984, bought a house at North Tawton and lived there from time to time until shortly before his death.

Marcia Willett (1945–), wrote several family sagas, including the Chadwick Family Chronicles trilogy, set mostly on Dartmoor and the South Hams area.

Nigel West, pseudonym of Rupert Allason (1951–), Conservative MP for Torbay (1987–97) and military historian, is author of several books on intelligence and security issues, and spy thrillers.

Michael Jecks (1960–) is author of the Templar series of West Country mysteries set on Dartmoor, and part-author of collaborative novels with fellow members of the Medieval Murderers.

Ian Mortimer (1967–), Dartmoor-based historian, author of several medieval histories and biographies, including *The Time Traveller's Guide to Medieval England,* and works on Edward III and Henry IV.

REFERENCES TO DEVON IN POETRY & SONG

'More discontents I never had
Since I was born, than here;
Where I have been, and still am sad
In this dull Devonshire.'
                    Robert Herrick, 'Discontents in Devon'

'Fairest maid on Devon banks,
Crystal Devon, winding Devon,
Wilt thou lay that frown aside,
And smile as thou wert wont to do?'
                    Robert Burns, 'Fairest maid on Devon banks'

'How pleasant the banks of the clear winding Devon,
With green spreading bushes and flow'rs blooming fair!
But the boniest flow'r on the banks of the Devon
Was once a sweet bud on the braes of the Ayr.

Mild be the sun on this sweet blushing flower,
In the gay rosy morn, as it bathes in the dew;
And gentle the fall of the soft vernal shower,
That steals on the evening each leaf to renew!
O spare the dear blossom, ye orient breezes,
With chill hoary wing as ye usher the dawn;
And far be thou distant, thou reptile that seizes
The verdure and pride of the garden or lawn!
Let Bourbon exult in his gay gilded lilies,
And England triumphant display her proud rose:
A fairer than either adorns the green valleys,
Where Devon, sweet Devon, meandering flows.'

Robert Burns, 'The Banks of the Devon'

'So Lord Howard past away with five ships of war that day,
Till he melted like a cloud in the silent summer heaven;
But Sir Richard bore in hand all his sick men from the land
Very carefully and slow,
Men of Bideford in Devon,
And we laid them on the ballast down below;
For we brought them all aboard,
And they blest him in their pain, that they were not left to Spain,
To the thumbscrew and the stake, for the glory of the Lord'

Alfred, Lord Tennyson, 'The Revenge'

''Tis eve! 'tis glimmering eve! how fair the scene,
Touched by the soft hues of the dreamy west!
Dim hills afar, and happy vales between,
With the tall corn's deep furrow calmly blest:
Beneath, the sea! by Eve's fond gale caressed,
'Mid groves of living green that fringe its side;
Dark sails that gleam on ocean's heaving breast
From the glad fisher-barks that homeward glide,
To make Clovelly's shores at pleasant evening-tide.'

Robert Stephen Hawker, 'Clovelly'

'Sweeter than the odours borne on southern gales,
Comes the clotted nectar of my native vales –
Crimped and golden crusted, rich beyond compare,
Food on which a goddess evermore would fare.

Burns may praise his haggis, Horace sing of wine,
Hunt his Hybla-honey, which he deem'd divine,
But in the Elysiums of the poet's dream
Where is the delicious without Devon-cream?'
                    Edward Capern, 'To Clotted Cream'

'And bound on that journey you find your attorney (who
started that morning from Devon),
He's a bit undersized and you don't feel surprised when
he tells you he's only eleven'
W.S. Gilbert, 'The Lord Chancellor's Song' from *Iolanthe*, Act II

'All ye lovers of the picturesque, away
To beautiful Torquay and spend a holiday
'Tis health for invalids for to go there
To view the beautiful scenery and inhale the fragrant air,
Especially in the winter and spring-time of the year,
When the weather is not too hot, but is balmy and clear.

Torquay lies in a very deep and well-sheltered spot,
And at first sight by strangers it won't be forgot;
'Tis said to be the mildest place in all England,
And surrounded by lofty hills most beautiful and grand.'
                    William McGonagall, 'Beautiful Torquay'

'Take my drum to England, hang it by the shore,
Strike it when your powder's runnin' low;
If the Dons sight Devon, I'll quit the port o'Heaven,
An' drum them up the Channel as we drummed them long ago.'
                    Sir Henry John Newbolt, 'Drake's Drum'

'Buy my English posies!
Kent and Surrey may –
Violets of the Undercliff
Wet with Channel spray;
Cowslips from a Devon combe –
Midland furze afire –
Buy my English posies
And I'll sell your heart's desire!'
                    Rudyard Kipling, 'The Flowers'

WHAT FAMOUS AUTHORS
WROTE ABOUT DEVON

Daniel Defoe (*c.* 1660–1731) described several county towns in *A Tour Through the Whole Island of Great Britain* (1724–6), although there is some doubt as to whether he actually visited them all, or relied partly on information from his friends who had, and were happy to save him the trouble. Devonshire was 'so full of great towns, and those towns so full of people, and those people so universally employed in trade and manufactures, that not only it cannot be equalled in England, but perhaps not in Europe.' He called Honiton 'a large and beautiful market-town, very populous and well built.' From Honiton, he continued:

> The country is exceeding[ly] pleasant still, and on the road they have a beautiful prospect almost all the way to Exeter (which is twelve miles). On the left-hand of this road lies that part of the county which they call the South Hams, and which is famous for the best cider in that part of England . . . they tell us they send twenty thousand hogsheads of cider hence every year to London, and (which is still worse) that it is most of it bought there by the merchants to mix with their wines which, if true, is not much to the reputation of the London vintners.

Exeter, he noted, was:

> Large, rich, beautiful, populous, and was once a very strong city; but as to the last, as the castle, the walls, and all the old works are demolished, so, were they standing, the way of managing sieges and attacks of towns is such now, and so altered from what it was in those days, that Exeter in the utmost strength it could ever boast would not now hold out five days open trenches – nay, would hardly put an army to the trouble of opening trenches against it at all.

Totnes he called 'a very good town, of some trade . . . They have a very fine stone bridge here over the river, which, being within seven or eight miles of the sea, is very large; and the tide flows ten or twelve feet at the bridge.' Plympton was 'a poor and thinly-inhabited town,' while Plymouth was 'indeed a town of consideration.' He recalled being at the latter town the year after the great storm (in other words, probably 1704), during August, 'walking on the Hoo [*sic*] (which is a plain on the edge of the sea, looking to the road), I observed the evening so serene, so calm, so bright, and the sea so smooth, that a finer sight, I think, I never saw.'

John Keats (1795–1821) came to Teignmouth for a couple of months in 1818 to nurse his dying brother Tom, and while he was there he wrote part of his poem 'Isabella, or the Pot of Basil'. He did not like Devon, writing to a friend Benjamin Bailey (13 March 1818) that he had had to wear a jacket for the last three days:

To keep out the abominable Devonshire Weather – by the by you may say what you will of Devonshire: the truth is, it is a splashy, rainy, misty, snowy, foggy, haily, floody, muddy, slipshod county. The hills are very beautiful, when you get a sight of 'em; the primroses are out, – but then you are in; the cliffs are of a fine deep colour, but then the clouds are continually vieing with them.

H.V. Morton (1892–1979), one of the first people to drive round England in the early days of motoring and write about his experiences, waxed lyrical about the virtues of Plymouth in *In Search of England* (1927), in which he said that:

Every boy in England should be taken at least once to Plymouth; he should, if small, be torn away from his mother and sent out for a night with the fishing fleet; he should go out in the tenders to meet the Atlantic liners; he should be shown battleships building at Devonport; he should be taken to the Barbican and told the story of the *Mayflower* and the birth of New England; and most important of all his imagination should be kindled by tales of Hawkins and Drake on high, green Plymouth Hoe, the finest promenade in Europe.

Bill Bryson (1951–), who had moved from his native America to live in North Yorkshire and decided he would take one last trip round Britain before moving back to his homeland for a while, visited Exeter, as related in *Notes from a Small Island* (1995). The city, he wrote, was 'not an easy place to love', and he remarked on how after the Second World War the city fathers were given 'a wonderful opportunity, enthusiastically seized, to rebuild most of it in concrete.' Restaurants posed a problem, at least for the customer looking for something modest that did not have 'Fayre', 'Vegan', or 'Copper Kettle' in the title, to say nothing of restaurant-less streets and 'monstrous relief roads with massive roundabouts and complicated pedestrian crossings that clearly weren't designed to be negotiated on foot by anyone with less than six hours to spare.' He also marvelled at the logic of being offered a single train ticket to Barnstaple for £8.80, or a return for £4.40, and was impressed by the Royal Clarence Hotel's offer of a special deal on rooms at £25 a night 'if you promised not to steal the towels.'

DEVON LOCAL HISTORIANS

Llewellyn Jewitt (1816–86), a Yorkshireman who spent much of his life in Derbyshire, was Librarian of Plymouth Proprietary Library from 1849 to 1853, and published a *History of Plymouth* in 1872.

Richard John King (1818–79) was Plymouth-born but spent most of his life at Crediton. He was a prolific author, lecturer and journalist on historical and literary subjects and his books include works on Dartmoor and Totnes.

Sabine Baring-Gould (1834–1924) was not only a historian, but a prolific writer of magazine articles, novels, short stories, poems, non-fiction, hymns (notably the words to 'Onward Christian Soldiers') and folksong collector. At one time he had more titles listed under his name in the *British Museum Library General Catalogue of Printed Books* than any other English writer. His best-known book remains *Devonshire Characters and Strange Events* (1908).

Richard Nicholls Worth (1837–96), born at Devonport, was a senior writer on the *Western Morning News* for several years, as well as author of works on Devonport, Plymouth and Devon. His son Richard Hansford Worth (1868–1950) shared his interests, though his first love was Dartmoor, and *Worth's Dartmoor*, the result of almost a lifetime's study, was published posthumously in 1953.

William Crossing (1847–1928), born in Plymouth, spent most of his life in South Devon, living for a while at South Brent, then Brentor, then Mary Tavy. His books on the moor, including *The Ancient Crosses of Dartmoor* (1887) and *A Hundred Years on Dartmoor* (1901), have regularly been reprinted and are still regarded as among the most authoritative on their subject.

Henry Francis Whitfeld (1853–1908), editor at various times of the *Western Daily Mercury* and *Western Independent*, published *Plymouth and Devonport in Times of War and Peace* (1900).

C.W. Bracken (1858–1950), headmaster of Plymouth Corporation Grammar School from 1909 until his retirement in 1930, published a *History of Plymouth* the following year, reprinted with a postscript by W. Best Harris (see p. 50) in 1970.

R.A.J. Walling (1869–1949), another journalist who worked on several senior newspapers, was for a while editor of the only Sunday local, *The Western Independent*. A prolific writer of books on the West Country and of detective novels, his most enduring work, *The Story of Plymouth*, was published a few months after his death.

W.G. Hoskins (1908–92), born in Exeter, taught local history at Leicester and Oxford and did much to achieve recognition for local history as a subject worthy of academic study. His *Devon* (1954), part of the New Survey of England series, remains a standard work on the county. His other titles include *The Making of the English Landscape* (1955), *Devon and its People* (1959), and *Two Thousand Years in Exeter* (1960). In 1976 he presented a BBC TV series, *The Landscape of England*.

W. ('Bill') Best Harris (1912–87), a Welshman by birth, came to Plymouth as Senior Assistant Librarian in 1935, and was City Librarian from 1957 to 1974. He regularly wrote, broadcast and lectured on the history of the area, his best-known title being *Stories from Plymouth's History* (1969). As a librarian he was naturally a passionate bibliophile. He once stopped three lorries taking books to a corporation refuse tip, bought the lot, and found several rare editions among the collections he had thus acquired.

Crispin Gill (1916–2004), born in Plymouth, assistant editor of the *Western Morning News* and later editor of *The Countryman*, made a lifelong study of the city in which he was born, publishing a two-volume history which was later reissued in one volume.

Chris Robinson (1954–), writer, artist and historian, has written and published several works on his home city, including *Victorian Plymouth*, *Plymouth in the Twenties and Thirties*, and *150 Years of the Co-operative in Plymouth*. He has also presented shows on local radio, and runs a studio gallery on the Barbican.

From the age of the internet, David Cornforth (Exeter Memories) and Brian Moseley (Plymouth Data) have published invaluable and regularly updated histories of their respective cities online.

DEVON PUBLISHERS

All counties have, or have had, several publishers ranging from prestigious firms to cottage industries. This list highlights a selection, including the best-known, local history in most cases being their speciality.

Arthur H. Stockwell Ltd, Ilfracombe. Established in 1898, this has proved the longest-lasting to date.

David & Charles, Newton Abbot. Established in 1960 by David S. John Thomas and Charles Hadfield, this firm rapidly acquired a reputation for its railway and canal histories in particular. It later acquired the Readers Union Book Club, and in 2000 it was acquired by F & W Media International Ltd.

Forest Press, Liverton.

Halsgrove, Wellington. Although having recently moved from Tiverton to Somerset, Halsgrove began as Devon Books, official publishers to Devon County Council, and as such synonymous with high-quality local history titles including the 'Community History' series on individual Devon towns and villages.

Macdonald & Evans, Plymouth, were acquired by Harper & Row in 1985 and became Plymbridge Distributors. The company went into liquidation in 2003 and was acquired by the US-based Rowman & Littlefield, later National Book Network International (NBNi).

Obelisk Publications, Exeter.

Orchard Publications, Chudleigh.

Paternoster Press, a Christian publishing company founded in 1936 in London, which later moved to Exeter and was acquired in 1992 by a Christian book distributor, Send The Light.

Reflect Press Ltd, Exeter.

University of Exeter Press.

Webb & Bower, Exeter. Established in 1975 by Richard Webb (a former publicity director for David & Charles) and Delian Bower, it was briefly one of the most successful firms in the country with the runaway success of *County Diary of an Edwardian Lady* (1977) by Edith Holden (1871–1920), a facsimile of a wildlife diary from 1906 published with the author's original watercolour illustrations. In 1991 the firm was scaled down and became Dartmouth Books.

Although not strictly publishers, some mention should be made of A. Wheaton & Co., one of the country's oldest firms, established in Exeter in 1780 by James Penny as a printer and bookseller. It was acquired by William Wheaton in 1835 and taken over after his death in 1846 by his son Alfred, hence the initial in the title. Despite the destruction of the premises on High Street in the Second World War, the company went from strength to strength. In 1965 it moved to a newly built site at Marsh Barton, and next year it was taken over by Pergamon Press, becoming in the process a specialist in producing school textbooks for the British market. The publishing division closed in 1991, but the printing division, now Polestar Wheatons, remains one of the largest printers of British educational and scientific works.

DEVON SAYINGS, EXPRESSIONS & BELIEFS

If you touch a robin's nest, you will have a crooked finger all your life.

If you destroy a colony of ants, you will always have bad luck. Ants are sometimes thought to be the remains of a fairy tribe.

Conversely, in the early nineteenth century, it was believed that people should kill the first butterfly they saw each year, if they wanted to avoid ill-fortune for the rest of the year. Fortunately, more enlightened attitudes now prevail.

If good apples you must have, the leaves must be in the grave (in other words, trees must be planted after the leaves have fallen).

If swallows fly high, it is a sign of good weather, but if they fly low, they are trying to avoid the coming storms.

To devonshire – to clear or improve land by paring off weed, stubble and turf by burning them and spreading them on the land. The expression is thought to date back to the early seventeenth century, but by Victorian times had been shortened to 'denshire' or 'denshare'.

Dandelion leaves boiled in water with stinging nettles and watercress make a tonic which will ward off all illness, and dandelion flowers picked on St John's Eve (23 June), hung in bunches around doors and windows, will repel witches.

If picked from a young man's grave on the night of a full moon, the yarrow is a powerful aid when used to help cast spells, or in working witchcraft.

In Coryton, farmers believed that it was unlucky to take peacock feathers indoors, but in other parts of Devon they were used for ornament and decoration, and were said to bring good luck.

A robin entering a house will bring misfortune with it.

When rooks build nests deep into a tree, close in to the trunk, it is a sign of an impending bad summer.

In February, if farmers found that their hens had stopped laying, the milk from their cows turned pale and thin, or if the butter lost its colour, the snowdrop would be blamed if any were found in the house.

Dartmoor people say that when a snowstorm begins, Widecombe farmers are plucking their geese, and that when the rivers sound loud at night, it is a sign that rain is on the way.

When a full moon comes on a Sunday, the weather in the following month will be bad on land and sea.

The periwinkle, 'sorcerer's violet', or 'blue button', was often used as an ingredient in love potions, and regarded as useful for calming hysterics in women. It was sometimes known as 'cut-finger' as it was a binder which would stem the flow of blood.

Fleas never infest a person who is close to death.

It is unlucky to go to sea in a ship that has no rats aboard.

Snake-cracking, or taking an adder by its tail and cracking it like a whip quickly to break its back, was once considered a popular sport on Dartmoor. If not done quickly enough, the 'cracker' would probably be bitten.

If a Devon maiden prunes the rose at Easter, on Midsummer Day she should pick a rose while the clock chimes twelve, fold it in white paper, and put it away safely in a drawer until new year's day. She should then fetch it when she gets up on 1 January, and if she finds it is still fresh, she must pin it to her bosom. The man she will marry will meet her that day, and he will try and touch the rose 'in a gentlemanly way' if invited to do so. If the unwrapped rose has died, the maid will probably not find a husband at all that year.

A yew tree at Stoke Gabriel would grant your wish if you walked backwards around it seven times.

If three crows were seen together in the Hartland area, they would bring bad luck.

Early in the year, during wet weather, parents in Kingsbridge would tell their children to keep away from muddy lanes until the cuckoo came and licked up the mud.

Fruit stains on tablecloths or linen cannot be removed, until the season for the fruit that caused the stain has passed.

Sewing on a Sunday is not the done thing, as 'every stitch pricks our Lord,' while scissors should not be used on the Sabbath either. Hair and nails should not be cut on a Friday.

Finally, and somewhat tangentially, if someone does a Devon Loch, they fail at something when they are very close to winning, usually in a sporting context. The expression comes from Devon Loch, a horse owned by Queen Elizabeth the Queen Mother which ran in the Grand National in 1956, and was the favourite to win until inexplicably falling over within 40 yards of the winning post. I say 'tangentially', as the animal appears to have had no connection with the county apart from his name.

DEVON DIALECT

Bay-spittle – honey
Crumpetty – crooked
Dashel – thistle
Frenchnut – walnut
Goocoos – bluebells
Goosegogs – gooseberries
Granfer Greys or chuggypigs – woodlice
Grockle – holidaymaker
Horse-long-cripple – dragonfly
Nointed – wicked
Onwriggler – unpunctual, or uneven
Oodwall – woodpecker
Pegslooze – pigsty
Quelstring – sweltering
Skimmish – squeamish
Smarless – smallest
Spuddling – struggling
Storrage – commotion
Devonshire dumplings – people of what are politely called 'roly
    poly proportions'

BLUNDELL'S SCHOOL, TIVERTON

Founded in 1604 from a legacy left by bachelor Peter Blundell,
a merchant who had made his fortune in the cloth trade, the
original premises were vacated when it moved to a much larger
site and several more buildings about a mile away on the outskirts
of the town in 1882. Now a co-educational day and boarding
independent school, it has 350 boys and 225 girls.

Famous alumni
Sir John Eliot (1592–1632), statesman and staunch defender of
    rights of parliament against Charles I, who was imprisoned and
    died in the Tower of London
John 'Jack' Russell (1795–1883), the 'sporting parson' and dog
    breeder after whom a terrier was named

Frederick Temple (1821–1902), the Archbishop of Canterbury
   who crowned Edward VII
Sir J.C. Squire (1882–1958), poet, essayist and literary editor
A.V. (Archibald) Hill (1886–1977), physiologist and joint winner
   of the 1922 Nobel Prize for Medicine
Vernon Bartlett (1894–1983), journalist, author and politician
John Wyndham (1903–69), science fiction author
Donald Stokes, later Baron Stokes (1914–2008), industrialist and
   chairman of British Leyland Motors
Christopher Ondaatje (1933–), businessman, philanthropist and
   author
Richard Sharp (1938–), former England Rugby Union captain,
   said to have been the one after whom Bernard Cornwell's
   fictional hero Richard Sharpe was named
George Pitcher (1955–), journalist, author and Anglican priest

Conversely, infamous alumni include:
Bampfylde Moore Carew (1693–1759), rogue, vagabond, imposter,
confidence trickster and self-proclaimed king of the beggars.

He was believed to have given up his way of life and settled down after a handsome win on a lottery, which bearing in mind his past history, was probably more than he ever deserved.

C.E.M. Joad (1891–1953), philosopher, pacifist and radio broadcaster, expelled from the Fabian Society in 1925 for sexual misbehaviour at the summer school and barred from rejoining for nearly twenty years, and a persistent fare-dodger on trains until caught travelling without a valid ticket in 1948 and fined £2. The latter disgrace ended his broadcasting career.

Miles Giffard (1926–53), aspiring schoolboy cricketer who longed to turn professional and resented his father's insistence on finding him more conventional employment. After one too many quarrels with his father, he battered him and then his mother unconscious, threw their bodies into a wheelbarrow and over the cliffs to die, and was hanged for murder.

Famous people who have taught at Blundells include:
Eric Gill (1882–1940), sculptor and typeface designer
Neville Gorton (1888–1955), Bishop of Coventry
C. Northcote Parkinson (1909–93), naval historian and author, of
   Parkinson's Law fame
Sir Stephen Spender (1909–95), poet, essayist and novelist
Grahame Parker (1912–95), cricketer and rugby footballer
Mervyn Stockwood (1913–95), Anglican Bishop of Southwark
Malcolm Moss (1943–), Conservative MP

DARTINGTON HALL SCHOOL, NEAR TOTNES

Founded in 1926 by Leonard and Dorothy Elmhirst, it was a co-educational boarding school which prided itself on its progressive methods, with a minimum of formal classroom activity and an emphasis on estate activities. At one time it had over 300 pupils. After negative publicity (including old pictures of the headmaster's wife in a top-shelf magazine), falling numbers and financial problems it closed in 1987.

Famous alumni
Ivan Moffat (1918–2002), screenwriter and associate producer
Lucian Freud (1922–2011), painter
Oliver Postgate (1925–2008), creator of children's TV
    programmes including *The Clangers* and *Bagpuss*

UNIVERSITY OF EXETER

University College of the South West of England was established
in 1922 and became a full university on receiving its royal charter
in 1955.

Famous alumni
Robert Bolt (1924–95), playwright and screenwriter
Frank Gardner (1961–), journalist and BBC security correspondent
J.K. Rowling (1965–), author of Harry Potter books

UNIVERSITY OF PLYMOUTH

Formerly Polytechnic South West, it became a university in 1992.

Famous alumni
Philip Payton (1953–), historian
Michael Underwood (1975–), TV presenter

LOCAL NEWSPAPERS

Several towns have their own newspapers. This list includes some
of the more general titles:

Evening Herald   *Express & Echo*
Sunday Independent   *Mid-Devon Gazette*
Western Morning News   *North Devon Gazette*
Herald Express   *South Devon Gazette*

LOCAL JOURNALS & MAGAZINES

Devon Life
Devon Today
Dartmoor News
Dartmoor Magazine

4

CRIME & PUNISHMENT

PRISONS CURRENTLY IN USE

Princetown prison, constructed between 1806 and 1809 and opened in the latter year, was built to hold prisoners from the Napoleonic Wars and the Anglo-American War of 1812. In 1851 it was reopened as a civilian prison but closed briefly in 1917 to be converted into a Home Office Work Centre for conscientious objectors released from prison. In 1920 it became a prison for some of the country's most serious offenders. It suffered some damage in January 1932 during a riot by inmates, one of whom was shot and injured before order was restored. In 2007 it housed 646 prisoners. Famous former inmates included Michael Davitt, founder of the Irish National Land League and Nationalist MP, and Éamon de Valera, third President of Ireland.

Channings Wood prison, Denbury, near Newton Abbot, built partly by contract and partly prison labour, was opened in 1974. An adult male Category C institution, in 2008 it housed 731 prisoners.

Exeter prison, opened in about 1850, holds male adults and young offenders on remand to local courts from Cornwall, Devon and West Somerset. In 2005 it housed 533 prisoners.

FORMER PRISONS

The above prison replaced an older building. Exeter was also home to the Devon County Prison for Debtors, which closed in

1855 when the last inmates were moved to the county prison. The building later became a barracks for the First Devon Militia, and after further changes of use was largely demolished in 1909. The remaining wing was converted into houses, while part of the site was used as a church and later as a carpet and furniture showroom. Exeter Guildhall also had cells for housing prisoners, being last used thus in 1887.

Plymouth's first prison, next to the Guildhall in Whimple Street, closed in the early nineteenth century. Millbay Prison was built to house French and American prisoners of war until they could be taken to Princetown.

Devonport prison, Pennycomequick, was completed and opened in 1849. After the passing of the Prison Act in 1877 which required all gaols to be passed to state control, it was closed the following year. All inmates were transferred to Plymouth Borough Prison, Greenbank, also opened in 1849. It was closed in 1930 and the remaining inmates were transferred to Exeter. The building was converted into headquarters for City of Plymouth Police.

EXECUTIONS AT EXETER

The earliest executions recorded at Exeter were those of Alured de Porta, Elias Poyfed, Richard Stonyng, Thomas Amener, and Roger Twate, on 29 December 1285, for their role in the murder of Walter Lechlade, Precentor of Exeter Cathedral, in November 1283. Porta has the dubious distinction of being the only Mayor of Exeter to be hanged for murder.

The last man to be hanged at Exeter for an offence other than murder was William Bissett, on 20 August 1830. Aged sixty-five, 'an unhappy and miserably degraded old man', he was convicted at Exeter Assizes for having had 'a certain venereal and carnal intercourse' with a dog on 11 June that year, accused by Margaret McGennis who claimed to have witnessed the offence at Newton Abbot.

The last convicted murderer to be hanged in public at Exeter was Mary Ann Ashford, on 28 March 1866, found guilty of poisoning her husband. Since public hangings were abolished by Parliament in 1868, the following were convicted of murder in Devon and hanged at Exeter Prison:

William Taylor, 11 October 1869
John MacDonald, 10 August 1874
William Hussell, 19 November 1877
Annie Tooke, 11 August 1879
William Williams, 28 March 1893
Edmund Elliott, 31 March 1909
George Cunliffe, 25 February 1913
James Honeyands, 12 March 1914
Frederick Brooks, 12 December
    1916
Cyril Saunders, 30 November
    1920
Ernest Moss, 7 December
1937

Ernest Moss was the last convicted Devon murderer to go to the scaffold, for battering his girlfriend Kitty Bennett to death with a shotgun at Woolacombe on 9 August 1937.

Gordon Trenoweth, who killed shopkeeper Alfred Bateman in Falmouth on Christmas Eve 1942, was the last man to be hanged at Exeter, on 6 April 1943. After his execution, the gallows were dismantled and taken to Jersey where they were used in one further execution about ten years later.

The last woman to be hanged for murder at Exeter was Charlotte Bryant of Dorset, convicted of poisoning her husband in 1935. She went to the gallows on 15 July 1936.

Thomas Eames, who stabbed his wife Muriel to death at their home in Plymouth on 27 February 1952, after she had told him she was leaving him for another man, was the last man in Devon to be put to death for murder. He was executed at Winchester on 15 July.

Brian Churchill, who stabbed Jean Agnes Burnett to death, a teenager whom he had been stalking for several months, on a bus journey in Exeter on 22 July 1952, was found guilty of murder on 30 October, and thus became the last person in Devon to be sentenced to death. This was commuted to life imprisonment three weeks later.

THE CULLOMPTON KILLER

In 1693 or 1694 Thomas Austin, a Cullompton farmer who had lived beyond his means for some time, turned to fraud and eventually highway robbery in an effort to try to discharge his debts. After robbing and killing one wealthy gentleman on the road, he had an argument with his wife, and went to visit his uncle and aunt, but only the latter was in the house. He attacked and killed her and her children, stole all the money he could find in the house, returned home and cut the throats of his wife and children. His uncle came after him, and had him brought to justice. He was arrested and found guilty of murdering his wife, aunt and seven children, and hanged.

THE LAST DUEL IN DEVON

The last challenge of pistols at dawn in the county was in 1833, when Dr Peter Hennis, an Irishman who had gained a reputation for his hard work during the cholera epidemic of 1832, was accused by Judge Sir John Jeffcott of spreading scurrilous gossip about him and his family. The practice of duelling was no longer strictly legal, but something of a grey area. They fought at Haldon Racecourse on 11 May, ironically ten days after Jeffcott had been knighted. Hennis was shot and wounded, died in agony about a week later, and was buried at St Sidwell's Church, where his grave can still be clearly seen. Jeffcott was advised to flee to Sierra Leone before he was arrested for murder. He returned home a year later and was charged but acquitted due to lack of evidence. He took up an appointment in Australia, and in 1837 he drowned while being transferred to a prison ship as part of his duties. His body was never found.

THE MUTINEER

Richard Parker, born at Exeter in 1767, was the ringleader of the mutiny at the Nore, off Sheerness, Kent, on board HMS *Sandwich* in 1797, for which he was court-martialled and hanged.

BABY FARMERS

Baby farmers were a particularly gruesome aspect of Victorian England, whereby women would advertise to take infants off the hands of young women, usually unplanned and illegitimate children who were inconvenient to have around. The 'farmers' would demand a generous fee for the little ones' upkeep, and then kill them. Two major cases occurred in Devon during this era, both leading to death sentences, although only one of the convicted parties went to the gallows.

In December 1864 Charlotte Winsor of Torquay offered to take little Thomas Harris, aged two months, off his mother, for a fee of 3s per week. Two months later Thomas's dead body was found tied up in a parcel lying beside the road. Mrs Winsor was found guilty of murder and sentenced to death, but this was commuted to life imprisonment. As she admitted to having committed similar offences in the past, she was very fortunate to escape the rope. One of her victims had been the child of her own sister, who promised to pay her £4 if she would dispose of it. The sister only paid £2, and Mrs Winsor had never spoken to her since.

On 17 May 1879 parts of the mutilated body of Reginald Hede, the illegitimate baby son of Mary Hoskins of Camborne, were found by labourers in the River Exe. When police came to question Annie Tooke, a widow of Exeter, who had 'adopted' him, and asked her to produce the baby, she initially said that somebody else had taken him away about a fortnight earlier. The mother was arrested and charged with murder, but her innocence was established and she was acquitted. The police suspected that Mrs Tooke was lying, and while in custody she confessed to having suffocated the baby with a pillow, and then cut him up with a wood chopper. Although she later withdrew this confession, she was found guilty of murder and hanged on 11 August.

THE MAN THEY COULDN'T HANG

John Henry George Lee (1864–1945), known to posterity as 'Babbacombe' Lee, or 'the man they couldn't hang', was unique in British crime history as the only man who survived three attempts to hang him for murder. He was charged with the killing of Emma Keyse, an elderly widow who had employed him as a live-in handyman, at her home, The Glen at Babbacombe, near Torquay, on 15 November 1884. He already had a police record for theft, and he was known to have a grudge against Mrs Keyse as she reduced his wages because he was lazy and unreliable. Although the evidence against him was largely circumstantial, he was found guilty at his trial in February 1885.

When he went to the gallows at Exeter Prison on 23 February James Berry, the executioner, made three attempts to hang him, but the trapdoor failed to open. As it was deemed inhuman to prolong his agony further, the sentence was commuted to life imprisonment. He was released in December 1907 and, eager to exploit his experience, he sold his story to a newspaper and received a large fee which precluded any necessity for him to seek work ever again. John Lee being a common name, there is some doubt about what eventually became of him, but it is generally believed that he emigrated to New York, settled there with his common law wife, and died there in 1945, aged eighty.

THE UNSOLVED MULTIPLE MURDER

One of Devon's most unpleasant murder cases, which involved the killing of three members of the same family, has never been solved. Around or soon after midnight on 12 June 1936, Emily Maye (seventy) and her unmarried daughters Joan (twenty-eight) and Gwyneth (twenty-five), who still lived with their parents at Croft Farm, West Charleton, were battered to death at their cottage. The gruesome discovery was made by Charles Lockhart, their live-in gardener, when he returned home late from a dance in the village. Emily and Joan were already dead, Gwyneth was still just alive but unconscious, and although rushed to hospital, she died a few hours later. Thomas Maye (seventy-one), husband and father of the victims, was found semi-conscious with severe injuries.

After he had recovered, he was charged with triple murder and sent for trial in November, pleading not guilty. The defence maintained that such injuries could not have been self-inflicted, and that the attack had been carried out by person or persons unknown. Maye was found not guilty and acquitted, although a few villagers suspected that he was a man of uncertain temper who might have been provoked into doing the deed. When he died in 1957, he was buried at West Charleton Church beside his wife and daughters.

TREASON

Plymouth-born Duncan Alexander Croall Scott-Ford (1921–42), of the Merchant Navy, was hanged for treason at Wandsworth Gaol after being convicted of supplying information to the Germans on the movement of shipping. Details of his trial were kept secret until after his execution. Newspapers reported that he had betrayed his country for £18 and paid the ultimate penalty, as a warning to other Merchant Navy sailors who might have been similarly approached. He was the youngest person ever to be executed in Britain under the Treachery Act.

Guy Burgess (1911–63), born in Devonport, was an intelligence officer and double agent, part of the 'Cambridge Five' spy ring that betrayed Western secrets to the Soviet Union during the Cold War. He defected to Moscow in 1951 and died an alcoholic twelve years later.

CYBERCRIME

Christopher Pile (1969–), an unemployed computer programmer from St Budeaux, Plymouth, known as 'the Black Baron', was jailed in 1995 for eighteen months in what was described as the first case of its kind in Britain under the Computer Misuse Act of 1990. He was found guilty at Exeter Crown Court of eleven offences, including creating two computer viruses and another piece of software which made viruses harder to detect. The damage caused, it was estimated, could run into several millions of pounds, and one company alone allegedly lost £500,000 because of his activities.

5

COUNTRYSIDE & ENVIRONMENT

THE COASTLINE

The Jurassic Coast, a World Heritage Site chartered in 2001, stretches for 95 miles, from Orcombe Point, Exmouth, to Old Harry Rocks, near Swanage, Dorset. The entire length can be walked on the South West Coast Path, which runs 630 miles from Minehead, Somerset, to Poole Harbour, Dorset.

Prawle Point near Salcombe is the most southerly part of Devon, while Foreland Point near Lynton is the most northerly.

DARTMOOR

Dartmoor, covering 368sq miles, or 14 per cent of the county's land mass, was created a National Park in 1951 under the 1949 National Parks and Access to the Countryside Act.

The highest point on Dartmoor, High Willhays (2,039ft above sea level), is not only the highest in the county, but also in Britain south of the Brecon Beacons.

Canonteign Falls, in the Teign Valley, is England's highest waterfall, with the falls descending almost vertically for 220ft.

EXMOOR

Exmoor, of which 29 per cent lies in Devon and 71 per cent in Somerset, covering in all 267sq miles and 34 miles of coast, became a National Park in 1954. Part of the North Devon coast within Exmoor has the highest sea cliffs and coastline in England. Great Hangman, near Combe Martin, has a cliff face of 820ft, and the hill is 1,043ft high.

PLACE-NAMES

The name Devon is said to be derived from *Dyvnaint*, a Celtic term meaning 'a deep valley dweller'. The Roman name for Exeter was *Isca Dumnoniorum*. *Dumnonia* was the area of ancient Britain corresponding roughly to present-day Devon, and the *Dumnonia* the British Celtic tribe who lived there, the name taken from the proto-Celtic root word *dumno-*, meaning 'deep' and 'world'. *Isca* is alternatively said to be a Latin word for river, or for 'river full of fish'. Other names thought to be Celtic in origin are *Barum* for Barnstaple, and *Penn* for Newton Abbot. *Sudtone*, probably Saxon in origin and meaning 'south town', became Sutton, the settlement around the harbour which developed into Plymouth.

Buckfastleigh is believed to be unique among British place-names in using exactly half the letters of the alphabet, and each only once.

An even longer place-name in the county is shared by two villages, both called Woolfardisworthy, the larger being in the Torridge district and the smaller near Crediton. The name is believed to mean 'Wulfheard's homestead', Wulfheard being a medieval Bishop of Hereford who died in about AD 820. It is now generally pronounced and sometimes spelt Woolsery.

Several local names contain the word *cott*, Anglo-Saxon for a small hut; *worthy* or *worthig*, an area of enclosed land; or *combe* or *coombe*, a valley or well-hidden place. Pennycomequick, Plymouth, comes from the Celtic *Pen-y-combe-gwyk*, or settlement at the head of the creek valley. Goosewell is said to be from the

Anglo-Saxon *goose-wealig*, or spring of the goose, though is more likely to be from the Celtic *cus-ughel*, or high wood.

The South Hams takes its name from 'ham', or low-lying meadowland.

CONSERVATION CHARITIES

Devon Wildlife Trust
Devon Bird Watching and Preservation Society
The Royal Society for the Protection of Birds and English Nature both have several reserves in Devon, including some of those listed below, and Butterfly Conservation has a branch in the county.

BUTTERFLIES

Between 2006 and 2010, sightings of between forty-one and fifty different species have been reported annually to the Devon branch of Butterfly Conservation. The full list for 2006, the best of these years, is as follows, with the most common first and the last five having been recorded only once. Some are classed as migrants which rarely appear in Britain and do not breed here, while the Large Tortoiseshell, once fairly common, is thought to be extinct in this country although still fairly widespread in Europe.

Red Admiral
Small Tortoiseshell
Brimstone
Peacock
Meadow Brown
Hedge Brown (Gatekeeper)
Painted Lady
Speckled Wood
Small Copper
Comma
Holly Blue
Clouded Yellow

Orange Tip
Green-Veined White
Large White
Pearl-Bordered Fritillary
Small White
Wall Brown
Wood White
Green Hairstreak
Dingy Skipper
Grizzled Skipper
Heath Fritillary
Small Pearl-Bordered
  Fritillary

Small Heath
Common Blue
Marsh Fritillary
Dark Green Fritillary
Brown Argus
Large Skipper
Silver-Studded Blue
Ringlet
High Brown Fritillary
Marbled White
Small Skipper
White Admiral
Silver-Washed Fritillary

Purple Hairstreak
White Letter Hairstreak
Chalkhill Blue
Grayling
Pale Clouded Yellow
Long-Tailed Blue
Brown Hairstreak
Swallowtail
Camberwell Beauty
Bath White
Essex Skipper
Monarch (Milkweed)
Large Tortoiseshell

Recent years have seen an increase in Devon of two of the rarest English butterfly species, the Small Blue (the country's smallest resident butterfly) and the Marsh Fritillary. The Small Blue has been bred from larvae taken from a colony in Torbay and introduced to another area nearby by the Torbay Coast & Countryside Trust. On Dartmoor, the Two Moors Threatened Butterfly Project was set up by Butterfly Conservation in partnership with the Dartmoor and Exmoor National Park Authorities to try to reverse the decline in numbers of the Marsh, High Brown and Heath Fritillaries, and the sites kept under observation reported a healthy recovery in all three, particularly the former.

DEVON WILDLIFE & NATURE RESERVES

Aylesbeare Common
Baggy Point, near Croyde
Berry Head, near Brixham
Braunton Burrows
Chapel Wood, near Braunton
Dawlish Warren, Exe Estuary
Hope's Nose, Torbay
Lady's Wood, South Brent
Lundy Island
Morwellham
Occombe Valley Woods, near Paignton
Otter Estuary
Prawle Point, near East Prawle
Slapton Ley, near Torcross
Stover Country Park, near Newton Abbot
Yarner Wood, near Bovey Tracey

LUNDY

The waters around Lundy, which had been a marine nature reserve for over twenty years, were officially recognised as Britain's first marine conservation zone under the Marine and Coastal Access Act, which became law in November 2009.

Lundy is renowned for its rich variety of bird life. There are 317 species on the list of those recorded on the island, with an average of 144 different species recorded annually between 1980 and 2005, the record year being in 1985 with 160 species. It is a popular breeding site for the Manx Shearwater as well as the traditional Lundy seabird, the Puffin. Several vagrant species from North America and Europe have been seen, including the only British sightings of the Ancient Murrelet, Bimaculated Lark, Common Yellowthroat and American Robin.

Towards the end of the twentieth century the number of Puffins on Lundy declined sharply, from more than 3,500 pairs in 1939 to less than 10 pairs in 2000, while the Manx Shearwater showed a similar fall in numbers. In 2003 the Lundy Seabird Project was launched, part of which was a £50,000 operation to exterminate rats on the island by placing thousands of specially designed and baited traps laid in a strategic grid across the island.

DEVON ZOOS & WILDLIFE PARKS

Buckfast Butterfly Farm and Otter Sanctuary, Buckfastleigh
Combe Martin Wildlife Park
Dartmoor Wildlife Park, near Sparkwell, Plympton
Paignton Zoo Environmental Park
Shaldon Wildlife Trust

DEVON NATURALISTS & SCIENTISTS

Thomas Savery (*c.* 1650–1715), born at Shilstone, near Modbury, and Thomas Newcomen (*c.* 1663–1729), born in Dartmouth, went into partnership as inventors of the first practical steam engine for pumping water.

John Lethbridge (1675–1759), a wool merchant from Newton Abbot, invented an underwater diving machine in 1715 – an airtight barrel or oak cylinder with a glass porthole, enabling the user to salvage valuables from wrecks off the seabed.

Thomas Fowler (1777–1843), born in Great Torrington, patented the first convective heating system, forerunner of the modern central heating system, and built one of the first calculating machines.

William Snow Harris (1791–1867), born in Plymouth, nicknamed 'Thunder and Lightning Harris', invented a successful system of lightning conductors adopted by the Royal Navy.

Charles Babbage (1791–1871), born in London but brought up largely in Teignmouth and Totnes, was a mathematician, inventor and mechanical engineer credited with inventing the first mechanical computer.

William Elford Leach (1791–1836), born in Plymouth, collected marine samples from Plymouth Sound and along the coast as a boy. An expert on crustaceans and molluscs, he became Assistant Keeper of the Natural History Department in the British Museum, and published several major scientific works, including his *Systematic Catalogues of the Specimens of the Indigenous Mammalia and Birds in the British Museum*, and *Synopsis of the Mollusca of Great Britain*.

George Parker Bidder (1806–78), 'the Calculating Boy', a precocious child mathematician, born in Moretonhampstead, later became a civil engineer, and was involved in helping to plan and construct railways, gas lighting and transatlantic cables at home and abroad.

William Carpenter (1813–85), born at Exeter, physician, invertebrate zoologist and physiologist, was noted most for his research into marine zoology. He also wrote *Use and Abuse of Alcoholic Liquors*, one of the first books to promote the fact that alcoholism is a disease.

Charles Bate (1819–89), Cornish by birth, spent most of his life in Plymouth. A dentist by profession, he contributed several papers to learned journals on the subject. Also known for his zoological expertise, he produced a *Catalogue of Crustacea in the British Museum Collection*.

The Revd William Keble Martin (1887–1969), Archpriest of Haccombe and Rector of Coffinswell until his retirement in 1949, spent 60 years writing and illustrating *The Concise British Flora in Colour*. It was published in 1965 when he was aged 88 and it became an instant bestseller.

W.N.P. Barbellion, the pseudonym of naturalist and diarist Bruce Cummings (1889–1919), born in Barnstaple. He worked in the Department of Entomology at the Natural History Museum, Kensington, but early in adult life he was diagnosed with disseminated sclerosis. Selections from his diaries, mixing scientific and personal observations, were published in *The Journal of a Disappointed Man*, a few months before his death.

H.G. (Henry George) Hurrell (1901–81), was a regular broadcaster with the BBC Natural History Unit, and took a leading part in various international ornithological congresses. He bought a property near Wrangaton, South Brent, where he and his family kept ravens, otters and pine martens and a grey seal, Atlanta (see p. 101) in order to study their behaviour more closely. His books included *Wildlife – Tame but Free* (1968), and a short animal novel *Fling, the Story of the Pine Marten* (1980).

Tony Soper (1929–), founded the BBC Natural History Unit, became its first film producer, and presented several wildlife documentaries and children's series on TV. He also wrote widely on wildlife subjects, and the success of his *The Bird Table Book*, reprinted many times since its appearance in 1965, resulted in him being dubbed Britain's 'Mr Birdwatch'. His other titles include *Wildlife Begins at Home* (1975), and *Discovering Owls*, with John Sparks (1995).

COUNTY WEATHER RECORDS

February is generally the county's coldest month, when the sea reaches its lowest temperature. There have been occasional exceptions, such as when -8.9°C (48°F) was recorded at Exmouth on 13 January 1987. A combination of frosty midwinter weather with clear and calm nights resulted in -15.0°C (5°F) at Exeter Airport on 24 January 1958.

July and August are the warmest months, producing an average daily maximum temperature of around 18°C (64°F). The Torbay area, which faces east, is normally the warmest area of the county. Extreme high temperatures are rare, being associated with hot air brought from mainland Europe on south-easterly winds and accompanied by strong sunshine. The county's highest temperature was on 3 August 1990 when 35.4°C (96°F) was recorded at Saunton Sands. Temperatures over 31°C (88°F) were registered at several locations in Devon on 29 June 1976, and of 33°C (91°F) at Killerton in July 1923.

Devon's worst weather disaster in terms of lives lost was on the night of 15/16 August 1952 – 9in of rain fell on Long Barrow, Exmoor, in twelve hours, while the swollen East and West Lyn rivers destroyed the centre of Lynmouth and claimed thirty-four lives. Ninety-three houses were destroyed or so badly damaged that they had to be demolished, as were twenty-eight bridges in the area.

DROUGHTS

According to D. St Leger-Gordon (*Portrait of Devon*, 1963), Devon is unlikely to run dry, as it has more rivers and streams than any other English county, and while several run into Devon from its neighbours on either side, none run out until reaching the sea. Nevertheless, the county has regularly been affected by severe droughts, particularly in the especially sunny years of 1921, 1933–4, 1959, 1975–6, 1984 and 1989–90.

Of these, that of 1976 was by far the worst. A long, hot dry summer in 1975 was followed by an unusually dry winter and spring the following year. Parts of the county had no rain at all throughout June 1976, and temperatures of 32°C, or 89.6°F, were recorded for fourteen consecutive days throughout southern England. Teignmouth had no measurable rain throughout the summer and tinder-dry woodland, moorland and heathland areas were devastated by fires. The drought peaked during the holiday season in July and August when demand for water was at its greatest. A Drought Act was passed, standpipes were installed in some areas, and no substantial rain was recorded until late September.

SNOWFALL

Devon has also experienced heavy snowfalls and blizzards, and recent history has proved that one should not pay too much attention to those who predict that climate change and global warming will consign such occurrences to the history books.

In March 1891 *The Times* reported that 'no such storm had visited the West of England within remembrance'. Winter came late that year, but between 9 and 13 March Devon and Cornwall were almost completely cut off from the rest of the country by conditions in which over 200 people and 6,000 animals perished. Temperatures fell below zero, trees were felled by violent gales, and snowdrifts up to 15ft high in places were reported. Ships were driven on to the rocks, roads were impassable, and trains were snowbound. A train travelling from Yelverton to Princetown was trapped by a large snowdrift and could not move overnight, with three crew and six passengers having to huddle up together in a carriage until they were rescued the next day by a farmer struggling to tend his sheep. The line subsequently remained closed for several weeks.

Devon had a white Christmas in 1927 when snow began falling on Christmas Day, the heaviest falls seen in the region since 1891. Within 24 hours, most of East Devon was experiencing 10ft drifts, while on Dartmoor they reached 16ft. Diners were eating at a Princetown hotel that night, some less aware than others that snow was piling up outside the building so quickly that they would be unable to leave that night, and next morning convicts from the prison had to dig out warders from their snowbound homes so they could report for duty.

Even worse was the winter of early 1947. Over 7in of snow fell across most of the county in late January, while people in villages on and near Dartmoor were faced with 20ft drifts, and the RAF had to make food drops to some stranded communities.

On 28 December 1962 blizzards were reported over Devon and Cornwall, with 15ft drifts by 30 December. These conditions persisted for several weeks, and on 4 February 1963 seventy lorry drivers had to take refuge overnight in a school at Whiddon Down between Exeter and Okehampton. On 17 February, after several hours of brilliant sunshine (and fear of floods due to sudden thawing), some roads across Dartmoor were able to open for the first time since the week of Christmas. On 2 March troops relieved a farm on Dartmoor which had been cut off by 20ft drifts for 66 days.

After several days of dry, frosty conditions, up to 10in of snow fell overnight on 15/16 February 1978. Within two days, gales and blizzard conditions had resulted in much of Devon being at a standstill, and on 19 February 13½in of snow fell at Exeter Airport, resulting in drifts of up to 24ft. For three days many areas were without electricity as power lines were down, the M5 Exeter to Bristol and all roads over Dartmoor were impassable for several days, and due to the transport network being paralysed, food and water had to be flown in to some more remote communities by helicopter. By 22 February a thaw was setting in, but some of the larger snowdrifts were still visible for several weeks afterwards.

Although it was a comparatively mild winter in 2004, parts of Dartmoor, Torbay and Plymouth had light snowfall on Christmas Day. Six years later, on 20 December 2010, the county had its heaviest snowfall since February 1978. Commuters were trapped on the A38 at Haldon Hill for several hours, many schools were closed, and postal and refuse collection services were suspended for some days. Due to low temperatures, a thaw did not set in for over a week in most areas.

FLOODING

Although less severe than the disaster at Lynton referred to on p. 77, in October 1960 Exeter had 15in of rain, about half the annual average. On 26 October, 2½in fell, causing the level of the River Exe to rise suddenly, and next day it burst its banks, flooding much of the city. The worst affected was Okehampton Street, with 6ft of water. Several other towns along the East Devon coastline, including Exmouth, Sidmouth and Budleigh Salterton, were also badly inconvenienced.

THE MET OFFICE

The United Kingdom's national weather service, formerly the Meteorological Office, was founded in 1854 as a small department within the Board of Trade. In 2003 it moved its headquarters to a purpose-built £80,000,000 structure on the outskirts of Exeter, and was officially opened on 21 June 2004.

DEVON & RENEWABLE ENERGY

A MORI (Market Opinion Research International) poll, commissioned by Regen SW, the renewable energy agency for the south-west, was taken from 218 interviews conducted from a representative quota sample of Devon residents aged sixteen and over, from thirteen different sampling points, in October 2004. It found that 86 per cent of those polled supported the use of renewable energy, and only 2 per cent opposed it. Support was reflected in high levels in favour of wind power (76 per cent), and biomass power (67 per cent). 47 per cent of respondents had 'no strong feelings' about the appearance of wind farms, and the remainder who expressed an opinion were fairly evenly divided, with 28 per cent saying they liked them, 24 per cent not. Quotas were set on rural and urban location, age, gender and work status to ensure a representative sampling.

NATIONAL TRUST PROPERTIES

A La Ronde, Exmouth
Arlington Court, near Barnstaple
Bradley, Newton Abbot
Buckland Abbey, Yelverton
Castle Drogo, Drewsteignton
Church House, Widecombe
Coleton Fishacre, near Kingswear
Compton Castle, Paignton
Elizabethan House, Plymouth
Finch Foundry, near Okehampton
Greenway, Galmpton, near Brixham
Killerton, near Exeter
Knightshayes Court, near Tiverton
Loughwood Meeting House, near Axminster
Lundy Island
Lydford Gorge, near Okehampton
Markers Cottage, near Exeter
Old Bakery, Branscombe
Overbecks, near Salcombe
Saltram, Plympton
Shute Barton, near Axminster

Watersmeet House, near Lynmouth
Wheal Betsy Engine House, near Mary Tavy

Dunsland House, near Holsworthy, a National Trust property, was completely destroyed by fire in 1967.

LOST DEVON HOUSES & COMMUNITIES

Hallsands was a thriving coastal village near Start Point in Victorian times and had a population of about 160 in 1891. Around that time dredging began offshore to provide sand and gravel for expansion of the naval dockyard at Keyham, Plymouth. Within a few years the level of the beach had dropped significantly, and part of the sea wall was washed away. In 1902 the dredging licence was revoked, but the levels never recovered. During the storms of January 1917, a combination of easterly gales and exceptionally high tides breached the village's natural defences, and by the end of the year only one house was still habitable. No lives were lost, but all the villagers had to move further inland.

Morwellham Quay and New Quay (not to be confused with Newquay in Cornwall) are small abandoned villages near Tavistock, on the east banks of the Tamar. They prospered during Victorian times with the mining industry, but once the mines were exhausted in about 1900 they were abandoned. Morwellham later became a heritage museum, while New Quay and surrounding area are protected under World Heritage status.

Hundatora was a medieval village to the south-east of Hound Tor, with four Dartmoor longhouses, as well as several smaller houses and barns. It was mentioned in the Domesday Book as belonging to Tavistock Abbey. Hutholes, a village near Widecombe-in-the-Moor, consisted of two longhouses and three outhouses. Both were abandoned in about 1350, either due to the worsening climate or the Black Death, or a combination of both.

Eggesford House, near Chulmleigh, built between 1820 and 1830, was home of the Earl of Portsmouth. Abandoned in 1911, it had become little more than a ruin within less than ten years.

Membland Hall, the home and estate of Edward Baring, 1st Baron Revelstoke, was sold off piecemeal after he fell into debt in the 1890s. The increasingly dilapidated structure was largely destroyed by fire about forty years later and the remains were dynamited in the 1960s. Most of the estate buildings have since been converted to private residences.

Oldstone, near Blackawton, the home of the wealthy Dimes family, was gutted by fire in 1895 and the estate gradually went to rack and ruin. Laura, one of the Dimes daughters, had eloped with and married Hugh Shortland, a solicitor, in 1884, much against the wishes of her parents who suspected he was after the family money. He told her he was going abroad on business immediately after the wedding so she returned home without having had any honeymoon, and a few days later she was found drowned in a pond on the estate. He was put on trial for her murder but acquitted, and despite his persistent efforts to have the case reopened on the grounds that somebody else had killed her, nobody was ever brought to justice.

DEVON CURIOSITIES
& FOLLIES

Haldon Belvedere, or Lawrence's Castle, Haldon Hill
This was originally built by Sir Robert Palk in 1788 as a centrepiece to his estates, and dedicated to the memory of Major General Stringer Lawrence, Commander of the British armies in India in the 1750s. Renovated in 1995 by the Devon Historic Buildings Trust, supported by English Heritage, it is one of the finest examples of this type of triangular tower in England.

Daymark, Dartmouth Harbour
Standing 80ft high, this octagonal granite tower was erected in 1864 by the Dartmouth Harbour Commissioners as a replacement for a chapel which had stood there for centuries to help guide sailors into the harbour entrance. It has no lighting, and would therefore only have been useful in daytime.

Charge of the Light Brigade Monument, Hatherleigh

The monument was erected by public subscription in 1860 on the moorland outside the town to the memory of Lieutenant-Colonel William Morris. He was a locally born man who fought in the Battle of Balaclava in the Crimean War, but was wounded and died in India from sunstroke four years later. It is a large obelisk with a bronze bas-relief at the front of the pedestal, showing Morris being carried from the battlefield.

Mamhead Obelisk

A 100ft Portland stone structure built between 1742 and 1745 by Thomas Ball, a merchant, above Mamhead House, near Haldon, 'out of a regard to safety of such as might use to sail out of the Port to Exon or any others who might be driven on the coast.'

Rhenish Tower, Lynmouth

Built in about 1858 by General Rawdon on the main street facing the sea. He intended to keep salt water there for use in baths in the house, and refined it a couple of years later with battlements. The original was destroyed in the Lynmouth floods of 1952, and the present building is a copy.

Triumphal arch, Filleigh, near South Molton

The arch was erected in about 1730 by Earl Fortescue on a hill leading to his estates at Castle Hill, and rebuilt in 1961 after the original had been destroyed by the weight of overgrown ivy.

Conduit, Brownston Street, Modbury

A gift from merchant Adrian Swete in 1708, consisting largely of a squared granite block with a pyramidal roof surmounted with a ball finial, it was provided to bring a supply of fresh water to the town, fed by the reservoir higher up the street and sourced from the Silverwell Spring. It was moved to the side of the road in 1874.

South Brent jubilee sundial

In 1897 a lamp post-cum-signpost with an inscription on the three-sided base marking Queen Victoria's diamond jubilee was placed in South Brent Square, at the junction of Station Road, Church Street and Plymouth Road. Over the years it became increasingly vulnerable to larger vehicles, and it was moved in about 1969, to the fury of some residents who saw it as a valuable traffic-calming device. It was moved to two successive sites in the village, first to Station Yard and then to Wellington Square, about a hundred yards away from the original site. The lamp post and signpost have been removed and a sundial has been added on the top of the base, on the other two sides of which have been added inscriptions for the silver and golden jubilees of Queen Elizabeth II in 1977 and 2002.

The Ten Commandments stone, Buckland Beacon

In 1928 Parliament rejected a move to adopt the proposed new Book of Common Prayer, regarded by some as a 'Popish trend'. To commemorate what was seen as a victory for Protestantism, the then lord of Buckland Manor, William Whitely of Wellstor, commissioned Mr W.A. Clement, a stonemason from Exmouth, to engrave the Ten Commandments from a prayer book on two large stones. The work began on 23 July 1928 and was completed on 31 August. During that time, Mr Clement stayed in a cowshed in the woods nearby, with only a candle for light, and a stream in which to wash and from which to obtain drinking water. The inscriptions were recut in the summer of 1995 by the Dartmoor National Park Authority.

Cornworthy Priory Gatehouse

The sole remaining structure of the Augustinian priory of nuns at Cornworthy, near Dartmouth, the smallest of three Devon convents, founded in the early thirteenth century and dissolved in 1537. There are remains of some walls to the south-east.

Wheal Betsy Engine House

Used for mining operations for lead, copper, silver, arsenic and zinc near Mary Tavy, this is the last standing engine house on Dartmoor. The army were given permission to demolish it in 1954, but it was saved after strong lobbying by campaigners and given to the National Trust, who have since restored it.

Brunel Pumping Station, Torre, Torquay

Built between 1846 and 1848 on the Torquay branch of the South Devon Railway between Devon and Exeter, it was intended as part of a system for the atmospheric railway which would work by the propulsive force of compressed air, but the project was abandoned without being completed. It is the only pumping station to survive intact. Others survive, with minor damage, at Starcross and Totnes, and all are listed buildings. The one at Totnes became part of a milk processing factory in 1934 and remained in use until 2007. When Dairy Crest, the owners, tried to sell it off for a housing development in 2008, a campaign led by *Top Gear* presenter Jeremy Clarkson succeeded in saving it from demolition.

DEVON WINDMILLS

Part of the structure of the following windmills can still be seen, although in most cases all that remains is a derelict tower and part of the base.

Little Rey, Brixham
Cliston Manor, Broadclyst
Warborough, Galmpton
Instow
Lundy Island
Long Burrow, North Whilborough
Bidna, Northam
Fernacombe, Paignton
Heanton, Petrockstowe
Yaddon Down, Torquay

A millennium windmill was designed to be built at Occombe Farm, Paignton, as part of a proposal put forward for the Occombe Heritage Farm, based on that of mills operating in Devon in the nineteenth century, but with computer-controlled variations in sail area according to wind strength. It reached no further than the planning stages.

THE HOUSE THAT MOVED

In 1961 the fifteenth-century Merchant House, which formerly stood at 16 Edmund Street, Exeter, was earmarked for demolition to make way for a new road scheme. As one of the oldest surviving houses in Exeter, antiquarians and archaeologists lobbied successfully for it to be saved, and the City Council provided £10,000 for it to be moved. Several weeks were spent in preparing the 21-ton structure, as it was criss-crossed with strengthening timbers, and iron wheels attached to hydraulic jacks were placed at each corner. Iron bolts, screws and supports could not be used as these would have resulted in damage to the original timbers. It was moved in stages, beginning on 9 December. Four days later, Edmund Street was closed to traffic so the house could be moved up the road on a 10-ton timber cradle, with air compressors driving the winches as it was slowly dragged on the rails, up the street. The operation was completed within twenty-four hours and the house, having been moved 295ft, was placed in its new position, treated for woodworm, and a leaded-light window that was taken to the museum before the move for safe keeping was reinstalled. It has been successively been home to an antique dealer, a gem dealer and a wedding dress shop.

DEVON CASTLES

Few of these survive in their entirety, and only fragments of Plymouth Castle in particular still remain. The twentieth-century Castle Drogo was the last built in England, a distinction it is unlikely to forfeit.

Affeton Castle, West Worlington
Bampton Castle
Barnstaple Castle
Berry Pomeroy Castle
Bickleigh Castle
Castle Drogo
Dartmouth Castle
Gidleigh Castle
Hemyock Castle, Cullompton
Kingswear Castle
Lydford Castle
Okehampton Castle
Plymouth Castle
Powderham Castle
Rougemont Castle
Tiverton Castle
Totnes Castle
Watermouth Castle, near Ilfracombe

SOME DEVON MUSEUMS

Appledore, Maritime Museum
Ashburton Museum
Barnstaple, Museum of Barnstaple and North Devon
Bideford, Burton Art Gallery and Museum
Bideford, Parsonage Museum
Bideford Railway Museum
Brixham Heritage Museum
Budleigh Salterton, Countryside Museum and Bicton Park
     Botanical Gardens
Budleigh Salterton, Fairlynch Museum
Budleigh Salterton, Otterton Mill Centre and Working
     Museum
Cullompton, Coldharbour Mill Working Wool Museum
Exeter, Bill Douglas Centre for History of Cinema and Popular
     Culture
Exeter, Royal Albert Museum and Art Gallery
Exeter, St Nicholas Priory
Exmouth Museum
Honiton, Allhallows Museum of Lace and Local Antiquities
Lifton, Dingles Fairground Heritage Centre
Okehampton, Museum of Dartmoor Life
Plymouth City Museum and Art Gallery
Plymouth, Merchant's House Museum
Sidmouth Museum
Tavistock, Morwellham Quay and Tamar Valley Trust
Tiverton, Museum of Mid-Devon Life
Topsham Museum
Torquay Museum
Torquay, Torre Abbey Historic House and Gallery
Totnes, Elizabethan House Museum
Umberleigh, Cobbaton Combat Collection

DEVON'S ROMAN FORTS

Sites of Roman forts have been found at or close to the following.

Alverdiscott	Bolham Hill
Broadbury Castle	Clayhanger
Colebrooke	Cullompton
Hembury	Ide
Killerton	Lapford
Newton Tracey	Moridunum, Woodbury Farm, near Axminster

Parts of the Roman wall at Exeter remain, particularly around Southernhay, and a substantial Roman baths complex was excavated below the present surface of Cathedral Close by the Exeter Museums Archaeological Field Unit between 1971 and 1976, thought to be among the most impressive of any similar Roman structure in Britain. Over 1,000 Roman coins have been discovered in the city, emphasising its importance as a trading centre, particularly around the first half of the fourth century, though none were dated after AD 380.

DEVON'S TOP 10 TOURIST ATTRACTIONS

The following list of popular spots was compiled in a survey by TalkTalk telecommunications group.

1.   Crealy Adventure Park, Exeter
2.   Babbacombe Model Village
3.   Kents Cavern, Torquay
4.   South Devon Railway, Buckfastleigh to Totnes
5.   Plymouth Gin Distillery
6.   Clovelly
7.   Buckland Abbey
8.   Newton Abbot Racecourse
9.   Rosemoor Gardens
10.   Blackpool Sands

STATUES

Excluding monuments and war memorials with generic figures of soldiers and sailors, mythological figures such as Britannia, and effigies, these are the major statues of famous people to be seen in Devon. Some of those in Exeter have been moved from their original sites to places considered safer, often as a result of vulnerability to enemy action during the Second World War.

Bideford
Charles Kingsley (1819–75) – quayside

Brixham
King William III (1650–1702) – quayside

Exeter
Sir Thomas Dyke Acland, MP (1787–1871) – under city wall
Sir Redvers Buller, VC (1839–1908) – junction of Hele Road and New North Road
William Reginald Courtenay, 11th Earl of Devon (1807–88) – Bedford Street
John Dinham (1788–1864) – Northernhay Park
Bishop Richard Hooker (1554–1600) – Cathedral Green
Stafford Northcote, Earl of Iddesleigh (1818–87) – Northernhay Park
Queen Victoria (1819–1901) – Queen Street (not surprisingly)

Plymouth
Isambard Kingdom Brunel – Pennycomequick
Sir Francis Drake (replica of that at Tavistock below) – the Hoe
King William IV – Royal William Victualling Yard

Tavistock
Sir Francis Drake – Plymouth Road

Tiverton
King Edward VII – Lowman Green

PLYMOUTH MONUMENTS & MEMORIALS

Plymouth is rich in monuments and memorials, particularly around the Barbican area. The following is a selection of those to be seen there.

Mayflower Steps and surrounding wall overlooking sea,
all wall-mounted tablets unless indicated otherwise:
Mayflower Memorial to the Pilgrim Fathers, who sailed on 6 September 1620, tablet and carved granite block in surface of pier placed on quay wall 1891.

Sir Humphrey Gilbert's voyage from Plymouth Sound for Newfoundland, 11 June 1583, unveiled 1983.

Sea Venture Memorial to ship which sailed to Jamestown, Virginia, 2 June 1609, with crew of 150, wrecked on Bermuda reef, tablet unveiled 1959.

Tolpuddle Martyrs, four of six Dorset farmworkers 'after exile in Australia' where they had been deported, landing at Plymouth on 18 March 1838, unveiled 1956.

Tory, pioneer ship in colonisation of New Zealand, which left Plymouth in May 1839, unveiled 1939.

Seaplane N.C.4 arrival at Plymouth Sound on completion of first transatlantic flight, 31 May 1919.

Embarkation of Queen Elizabeth II and Prince Philip, Duke of Edinburgh, from quay on their visit to Plymouth, 26 July 1962.

Plaques on opposite wall
Memorial to Australian Settlers, transport ships *Friendship* and *Charlotte*, for convicts who sailed for Australia, 13 March 1787 and landed at Port Jackson, New South Wales, 26 January 1788, unveiled 1987.

Memorial to Cornish Emigrants who sailed for South Australia in the nineteenth century, unveiled 1986.

Memorial to Plymouth men who helped to found modern Australia, including Captain Tobias Furneaux, Captain John MacArthur, Captain William Bligh, Colonel George Arthur and Major Edmond Lockyer.

Memorial for sailing of six Plymouth Company vessels between 1840 and 1842 carrying settlers from Devon, Cornwall and Dorset to establish settlement of New Plymouth in New Zealand, unveiled 1988.

Fishing Boat *Dawn Waters* Memorial, crew of five from Devon and Cornwall who drowned when vessel sank off the Isle of Man, 20 March 1986.

To people of Plymouth from members of 10 Squadron, Royal Air Force, who operated from Mount Batten 1939–45.

Merchant Navy Memorial, to the 31,442 merchant seafarers who died in war and peace 1939–45.

The RNLI shop on the same side has a number of plaques commemorating individuals, including several lost at sea, or members of individual families. One is to Win and Fred Binney, who died in 1998 and 2002 respectively, inscribed 'Barbican people both died at 90 – it must have been all that fish'. Another is in memory of the six crew of MFV (Motor Fishing Vessel) *Pescado*, which sank off the Cornish coast on 28 February 1991 with the loss of all six crew, two of whom came from Plymouth.

Memorials and monuments on or near Plymouth Hoe
'Blitz', the Dog Mascot Memorial Cross, Hoe Park (see p. 101).

Sir Francis Chichester Memorial, West Hoe, memorial marking the spot where he came ashore on 28 May 1967 after his circumnavigation of the world, unveiled in 1997 by Prince Philip, Duke of Edinburgh.

Death by firing squad – cross embedded in pathway between Citadel Road and the Promenade, where three royal marines were executed on 6 July 1797 after being found guilty of incitement to mutiny among men at Stonehouse Barracks.

National Armada Memorial, unveiled 21 October 1890 by Prince Alfred, Duke of Edinburgh.

Smeaton's Tower, removed from Eddystone Rock and erected 1882.

South African (Prince Christian Victor) War Memorial, commemorating those killed in the Boer War, and to Queen Victoria's grandson who died of fever on the campaign, unveiled 1903.

Norrington Fountain, presented by Charles Norrington, Mayor of Plymouth, in memory of his wife who died in 1881, unveiled that same year.

Plymouth Naval Memorial, unveiled in 1924 by Prince George, later Duke of Kent.

Plymouth War Memorial, unveiled in 1923 by Lord Derby, Secretary of State for War.

Prejoma Clock, erected in 1965 under the terms of the will of Preston John Ball, in memory of his parents John and Mary, with the name taken from the initials of each Christian name.

Royal Air Force and Allied Air Forces Monument, unveiled in 1989 by Air Marshal Sir John Curtiss.

Reform Tablet, commemorating the passing of the Reform Bill in 1832, erected in 1833 near Belvedere, later removed to a wall in Madeira Road.

Royal Marine Memorial, unveiled in 1921 by Earl Fortescue, Lord Lieutenant of Devon.

*Memorials and monuments in Garden of Remembrance,
below the Belvedere, Plymouth Hoe*
1940 Dunkirk Veterans' Association Memorial.

Burma Star Association's Memorial.

Korean Veterans' Memorial.

Malayan and Borneo Veterans' Memorial.

Normandy Veterans' Memorial.

Plymouth Falklands Maritime Memorial, unveiled 1988.

Polis Naval Memorial, unveiled 1950.

In and around Devonport
Devonport Column, Monument Street, designed by Foulston,
completed in 1827.

Devonport World War Two Heroes' Memorial, North Corner,
Devonport.

Devonport War Memorial, Devonport Park, unveiled in 1923.

HMS *Doris* gun, Devonport Park, gun captured from Boers in
South African War and returned on board ship, unveiled in 1904.

Napier Fountain (Sir Charles Napier), Devonport Park, erected in
1863.

St Mark's Church War Memorial, now in Stoke Damerel Parish
Church.

Scott Memorial (Sir Robert Falcon Scott), Mount Wise,
Devonport, unveiled in 1925.

Memorials and monuments elsewhere in Plymouth
Charles Church. After the church was ruined in the blitz, the
City Council Reconstruction Committee intended to acquire

and demolish the remaining walls, but the Old Plymouth Society campaigned for its retention as a permanent memorial to the civilian dead of the Second World War, and it was dedicated thus by the Lord Mayor who unveiled a plaque on the north wall in 1958.

Charles Darwin and HMS *Beagle*, Devil's Point, East Stonehouse, a circular plaque marking the sailing of Darwin's ship on 27 December 1831 from Barn Pool, on the Cornish side of Plymouth Sound.

D-Day Memorial, Hooe Green, Plymstock, Dartmoor granite stone to which is affixed a plaque commemorating the embarkation of the United States Army, 29th Division, from Turnchapel to lead the Normandy landings on 6 June 1944.

HMS *Ark Royal* anchor, at junction of Armada Way and Notte Street. A Devonport-based ship, she was decommissioned in 1979 and the anchor was presented to the City of Plymouth.

Honicknowle War Memorial, Butt Park Road, removed from Honicknowle Methodist Chapel after it was closed, affixed to a wall outside Warwick Park House Nursing Home and unveiled in 1999.

Laira Great War Memorial, Old Laira Road.

Normandy Landings Memorial, Saltash Passage, St Budeaux, unveiled in 1958 by John Hay Whitney, US Ambassador to Britain.

Castle Green War Memorial, Plympton St Maurice, unveiled in 1924.

Burrow Hill War Memorial, Plymstock.

Portland Square Memorial Sculpture, Portland Building, University of Plymouth, dedicated to seventy-six men, women and children who were killed when part of the public air raid shelter in Portland Square was hit on the night of 22/23 April 1941, the worst civilian loss of life in a single bombing incident during the war. It was unveiled by Barbara Mills, one of the survivors, who had lost her parents, sister and grandfather in the attack.

Post Office Workers' Great War Memorial, Old Post Office Sorting Office, Central Park Avenue, dedicated to twenty-nine men 'particularly identified with the Plymouth office', unveiled in 1920.

Regent Brewery Great War Memorial, Union Street, East Stonehouse, dedicated to workers of the breweries lost in the First World War, unveiled in 1920.

Royal Air Force Mount Batten War Memorial, on side of Mount Batten Air Station, a replica propeller from a Sunderland flying boat.

St Andrew's Cross, 70ft high, erected outside St Andrew's Church as a memorial to the dead buried in the graveyard after it was levelled in 1884 and the remains transferred to the Westwell Street burial ground. It was badly damaged in the blitz and the remains were demolished a few months later. The surviving statues were transferred to the Guildhall, and the bronze cross which stood at the top is now on the main altar inside the church.

Sabbath Day Fight 1643 Memorial, Freedom Park, Greenbank, commemorating the Parliamentarians' victory over Prince Maurice's Royalist army.

South Atlantic Forces Memorial, Booking Hall, North Road Railway Station, commemorating those who fell in the Falklands War, and incorporating crests representing all the armed services who took part in the campaign.

Tamerton Foliot War Memorial, St Mary's Church.

Z4 Secret Radar Unit Memorial, Ridge Cross, Brixton, commemorating the work of the secret radar unit of 144 heavy anti-aircraft rocket battery, code name Z4, who would detect approaching German bombers, unveiled in 2009.

EXETER MEMORIALS

Livery Dole Martyrs' Memorial, on the corner of Barnfield Road and Denmark Road, in memory of two Protestant martyrs of the Tudor era who died at the stake, Thomas Benet in 1531, for denying the supremacy of the Pope, and Agnes Prest in 1557, for refusing to accept the doctrine of transubstantiation.

Guildhall Boer War Memorial.

St Hele's School Boer War Memorial, St David's Church.

Blue Boy, a statue cast in 1636 which has been extensively restored over the years, originally stood at the entrance to St John's Hospital School and was moved to Princesshay. When the latter was refurbished in 2007, it was moved again and placed on a new plinth.

Volunteer Force Memorial, Northernhay Gardens, commemorating the founding of the Volunteer Force in 1852, unveiled in 1895.

World War One Memorial, commemorating and inscribed with names of the 187 buried in Higher Cemetery, situated near entrance to St Mark's Avenue.

World War Two Memorial, a cross surrounded by blocks of graves in Higher Cemetery.

TORQUAY MEMORIALS

10th Battalion Home Guard Memorial, Corbyn Head, Torquay, commemorating the Home Guard, Torbay, and the Corbyn Head tragedy when five members died after their anti-aircraft gun exploded in 1944.

Churchill Memorial Gardens, Berry Head Road, Brixham.

Churston War Memorial, Churston Common, Brixham.

Churston War Memorial Playing Field, Greenway Road, Brixham.

Harrison Memorial, Roundham Head, Paignton, stone of remembrance with tablet dedicated to Lieutenant Commander Arthur Harrison, VC (1886–1918), killed during the Zeebrugge raid, April 1918.

Memorial Gardens, Union Street, Torquay.

Old Parish Church, Torre, Torquay, containing memorial stones and white war crosses in remembrance of deceased members of the parish.

Palace Avenue War Memorial, Palace Gardens, Paignton, memorial at eastern end.

Princess Gardens Memorial, Torbay Road, Torquay.

DEVON CEMETERIES

Plymouth
Efford Cemetery
Weston Mill
Ridge Cross, Plymstock
Milehouse
Jewish Cemetery, Compton Gifford
Ford Park
Drake Memorial Park, Plympton St Mary

Exeter
Bartholomew's Yard
Catacombs and Lower Cemetery
Higher Cemetery
Exwick Cemetery

Torquay
Torquay Crematorium and Cemetery

DEVON RESERVOIRS

Avon Dam, Dartmoor
Burrator, Dartmoor
Challacombe, Exmoor
Darracott, near Torrington
Fernworthy, Dartmoor
Holywell, near North Molton
Jennetts, Barnstaple
Kennick, Dartmoor
Melbury, near Bideford
Meldon, near Okehampton
Roadford, near Bratton Clovelly
Slade, near Ilfracombe
Tottiford, Dartmoor
Trenchford, Dartmoor
Venford, Dartmoor
Wistlandpound, Exmoor

DEVON ISLANDS

A look at Ordnance Survey maps will reveal numerous tiny islands, in most cases no more than rocks (sometimes named), off Devon's coasts. In addition to these are what may be called the six main islands, although for the most part they are only inhabited by wildlife. Before anyone comes to the wrong conclusion, the Shag Stone is named thus as it is much favoured by seabirds, especially cormorants and shags.

Lundy, at about 3 miles by ¾ of a mile at the widest point the largest, 12 miles off the coast of North Devon.

Burgh Island, off Bigbury-on-Sea.

Drake's Island, formerly St Nicholas's Island.

Great Mewstone, off Wembury Point, Plymouth.

Shag Stone, near eastern entrance to Plymouth Sound.

Thatcher's Rock, off Torquay.

DEVON'S TOP 10 BIRDS

The 2010 Big Garden Birdwatch, organised by the Royal Society for the Protection of Birds in association with the BBC, used viewers' returns to compile a league table of the most frequently seen birds in people's gardens. The previous year's position is in brackets.

  1 (1) House sparrow – 3.79
           pairs per garden
  2 (3) Blackbird – 2.87
  3 (2) Chaffinch – 2.77
  4 (5) Blue tit – 2.70
  5 (-) Long-tailed tit – 1.81
  6 (4) Starling – 1.74
  7 (8) Great tit – 1.59
  8 (7) Robin – 1.51
  9 (9) Wood pigeon – 1.45
10 (6) Greenfinch – 1.41

The absentee from this list, no. 10 in 2009, is the Goldfinch.

Devon's county bird in effect is the Dipper, seen on rivers and streams, the emblem of the Devon Trust for Nature Conservation. It has since been superseded by the Devon Wildlife Trust, which has the face of a badger as part of its masthead.

In addition to the birds occasionally recorded on Lundy (see pp. 72–4), Devon has recently been host to other rare species. The south coast is the last stronghold of the scarce Cirl Bunting. The Red-Backed Shrike, which had last been recorded as breeding in Britain in the early 1990s in East Anglia, returned to breed in Dartmoor in summer 2010. Two birds which breed in North America and Canada and are classed as occasional British migrants have been seen in recent years, Wilson's Phalarope on the coast near Topsham in 2009, and Bonaparte's Gull over the River Otter in 2011. Early that same year an American Purple Gallinule, which had previously been recorded only three times in Britain, was found (unfortunately dead) in Tavistock.

FAMOUS ANIMALS

Blitz

Blitz was a black and tan mongrel puppy that ran into the ARP Rescue Depot in Mill Street, Plymouth, during an air raid in 1941, and the rescuers promptly adopted him as their mascot. One of them recalled years later that he would sit in a rocking chair at the depot, keeping an eye on them. They were all so tired after a day's work that they would nod off as soon as the Commanding Officer got his head down, but as soon as anything stirred in the yard, Blitz would growl and paw at their heads to wake them up. It was also claimed that he would help to find people trapped in the debris after buildings were destroyed. He was run over by a lorry and killed in August 1942. Some carpenters made him a small oak coffin and a small memorial cross, placed outside the old depot, was later removed to The Hoe. The original and a replacement have been stolen but subsequently replaced.

Atlanta

Atlanta was a starving Atlantic grey seal pup that was rescued by two fishermen in November 1959 after being stranded on the Yealm estuary during very stormy weather. Naturalist H.G. Hurrell (see p. 76) took charge of her and gave her a home in the swimming pool in his garden at Wrangaton, near South Brent. She was taught to respond to verbal instructions and intelligence tests, including putting letters and numbers on large signs in order. Thousands visited Moorgate every year to come and see her, including a schoolboy in Vancouver about to make his first visit to Britain who said what he wanted to see most of all was Mr Hurrell's seal and the London Underground. She died in 1973. He wrote about her in *Atlanta my Seal* (1963).

Casper

Casper was a black and white cat that lived in Plymouth and had been acquired by his owner Susan Finden, of St Budeaux, as a rescue cat in 2002 and became world famous as a bus commuter. She named him Casper after the friendly ghost. He would get on a bus at a stop for the No. 3 First Devon and Cornwall service outside the front door at his home around 10 a.m. each morning and curl up on a seat throughout the full 11-mile route to the city centre, travelling for up to an hour before arriving back at the same stop. She was amazed when she found out he had become a regular passenger. Drivers on the service were advised to look out for him and ensure he got off at the right point. During five years he travelled an estimated 20,000 miles on the bus, was featured on local television, and when it was uploaded on to Youtube he achieved worldwide fame. He was killed on 14 January 2010, aged twelve, by a hit-and-run driver while crossing the road for his daily journey.

DEVON RIVERS

Ashburn
Rises on Horridge Common near Rippon Tor, flows down a steep river valley through woods and under stone bridges before entering Ashburton and joining the River Dart near Buckfastleigh.

Avon, or Aune
Rises in a boggy area near Ryder's Hill, leaves Dartmoor at point where Avon Reservoir was built and completed in 1957, passes through South Brent, Avonwick and Aveton Gifford, and flows into the sea at Bigbury Bay.

Axe
Flows through Dorset and Somerset as well as Devon, rising near Beaminster, Dorset, flows west and then south through Axminster and into the sea at Axmouth, being fed by several streams and by tributaries Yarty and Coly.

Barle
Rises in the Somerset area of Exmoor, joining the River Exe at Exebridge, on the Devon/Somerset border.

Batherm
Flows through Somerset and Devon, joining the River Exe downstream near Bampton.

Clyst
Rises near Clyst William, near Cullompton, runs rest and south-west through Clyst Hydon, Clyst St Lawrence, Westwood, to Clyst Valley, then south through Broadclyst, West Clyst, Clyst Honiton, Clyst St Mary, Clyst St George, and into the Exe Estuary at Bowling Green Marsh, south of Topsham.

Culm
Rises in the Blackdown Hills, flows west through Hemyock, Culmstock, Uffculme, turns south and flows through Cullompton, alongside the M5 motorway, and the northern boundary of Killerton Park, to join the Exe below Stoke Canon.

Dart
The river which gives Dartmoor its name begins as two tributaries – East Dart, its source south of Cranmere Pool, flowing south to Postbridge and past Bellever, and West Dart, its source near Lower White Tor, flowing south to Two Bridges and then south-east past Hexworthy. East and West Dart join at Dartmeet, where the resulting single river is crossed by several ancient clapper bridges, then the Dart leaves the moor and flows southwards past Buckfast Abbey, through Buckfastleigh, Dartington and Totnes, where it becomes tidal. Kingswear is on the east of the estuary, and Dartmouth on the west. The Dart's tributaries include the Cowsic, Blackbrook, Swincombe and O Brook on the right bank, and Cherry Brook on the left.

Erme
Rises in southern Dartmoor on Abbot's Way near River Plym, flows southerly through Ivybridge, past Ermington and Modbury, entering the English Channel near Kingston. The Wonwell and Kingston beaches lie at the mouth of the river on the Erme Estuary.

Exe
The river after which Exeter is named rises near Simonsbath, Exmoor, in Somerset, but flows south and most of it is on the Devon side of the county border. Exmouth is on the east of the estuary mouth, Dawlish Warren on the west, while its tributary the Creedy gives its name to Crediton.

Heddon

Running along the west of Exmoor, reaching the North Devon coast at Heddon's Mouth.

Lemon

Rising near Haytor, Dartmoor, it joins Langworthy Brook, Sigford, passes the village of Bickington, then flows through the woods in Bradley Valley, through Newton Abbot, and joins the River Teign near the head of its estuary.

Lew

A name shared by two short rivers. The more northerly, giving its name to Northlew, rises south of Beaworthy, flows east, turns north and flows past Hatherleigh and joins River Torridge. The southerly river rises near Surton, north Dartmoor, flows west and south through Lew Valley past Lewtrenchard, south of Lewdown, then joins the River Lyd near Marystow, or Stow St Mary.

Lyd

Rising at Lyd Head, Dartmoor, flowing into the River Tamar near Lifton. Its most spectacular feature is the 1½ mile-long Lydford Gorge.

Meavy

Forming an outlet from Burrator Reservoir, it flows south-west past Meavy and south, then joining the River Plym at the upper end of Bickleigh Vale.

Otter

Rising in the Blackdown Hills, on the Somerset side of the border, flows south through East Devon, though and by Upottery, Rawridge, Monkton, Honiton, Alphington, Ottery St Mary, Tipton St John, Newton Poppleford, Otterton, reaching the coast to the east of Budleigh Salterton, and into the English Channel at western end of Lyme Bay. The River Tale is a small tributary.

Plym

Rising at a small spring, Plym Head, southern Dartmoor, the river flows south-west to Plymouth where it enters the sea.

Sid

Flowing from its source in Crowpits Covert, it flows south through Sidbury and Sidmouth and into the English Channel.

Tamar

Forming most of the border between Devon and Cornwall, it flows south and into the Hamoaze before entering Plymouth Sound. Its Devon tributaries include the Tavy and Deer. The Tavy has its own tributaries, the Collybrooke, Burn, Wallabrook, Lumburn and Walkham.

Taw

Rising at Taw Head, northern Dartmoor, it reaches the Bristol Channel at a joint estuary mouth with the Torridge. Its tributaries are the Little Dart, the Mole and two different rivers named Yeo, known as the Lapford Yeo and the Barnstaple Yeo respectively.

Teign
Rising near Cranmere Pool, Dartmoor, it flows southwards at the eastern edge, beneath Castle Drogo, becomes tidal at Newton Abbot, and flows into the English Channel at Teignmouth.

Thrushel
Runs westerly from its source near Meldon to Tinhay, where it joins the Wolf.

Torridge
Rising close to the border with Cornwall, it flows east, between East Putford and West Putford, and near Bradford, where it is joined by the Waldon, then east past Black Torrington and Sheepwash to Hatherleigh, where it is joined by the Lew, and then the Okement, then northwards past Little Torrington and Great Torrington, and into the estuary at Bideford. Between Appledore and Instow it joins the Taw Estuary. Its tributaries are the Ockment, or Okement, where the East and West Okement join at Okehampton and flow north past Jacobstowe and Monkokehampton before joining the Torridge near Meeth.

East Webburn
Rising on West Dartmoor, south past Widecombe-in-the-Moor and joining the West Webburn, they join the River Dart near Holne.

Wolf
Runs from Broadbury and into Roadford Lake Reservoir, through Slew Woods, below Broadwoodwidger, and continues south, merging with the Thrushel near Stowford, joining the Lew at Tinhay near Lifton and becomes the Lyd, which later joins the River Tamar at the Devon-Cornwall border east of Launceston.

Yealm
Rising on the Stall Moor mires, southern Dartmoor, passes through Cornwood, Lee Mill and Yealmpton, and reaches the estuary mouth below Newton Ferrers and Noss Mayo.

DEVON GARDENS

Some of these have also been listed under other categories, such as National Trust properties, but are still noteworthy as among the county's finest gardens in their own right. Paignton Zoo, first opened in 1923, was one of the earliest combined zoological and botanical gardens in Britain, and the first that was opened with education as its mission.

Abbey Park, Torquay
Arlington Court Gardens, Barnstaple
Bicton Park Botanical Gardens
Brunel Manor Gardens, Torquay
Brunel Woods
Buckland Abbey Gardens, Yelverton
Burrow Farm, Dalwood, Axminster
Castle Drogo, Drewsteignton
Castle Hill, Filleigh, Barnstaple
Clovelly Court Gardens
Cockington Court & Country Park, Torquay
Coleton Fishacre, Kingswear
Connaught Gardens, Sidmouth
Garden House, Buckland Monachorum
Killerton Gardens, Broadclyst
Knightshayes Gardens, Tiverton
Marwood Hill Gardens, Barnstaple
Overbecks, Salcombe
Paignton Zoo Environmental Park
Pecorama Pleasure Gardens, Beer
Princess Gardens, Torquay
Romaleyn Gardens, Paignton
Rosemoor Gardens (RHS), Great Torrington
Royal Terrace Gardens, Torquay
Saltram, Plympton
Stone Lane Arboretum, Chagford
Tessier Gardens, Babbacombe
Tiverton Castle Gardens
Torre Abbey Gardens, Torquay

DARTMOOR ANCIENT TENEMENTS

Ancient tenements are the oldest surviving Dartmoor farms, established in the thirteenth and fourteenth centuries on sites where settlers were allowed to build farms, and release their livestock to graze on the surrounding land. The following are still in existence today, and most still feature buildings of medieval origin, including elements of their original longhouses. Most are Grade II listed buildings.

Babeny	Huccaby
Bellever	Lakehead
Brimpts	Merripit
Brownberry	Pizwell
Dunnabridge	Prince Hall
Dury	Riddon
Hartyand	Runnage
Hexworthy	Sherberton

DARTMOOR BRONZE AGE STONE CIRCLES

Stone circles, meeting places in the Bronze Age, were located at mutually agreed areas between the well-defined boundary systems on the moor, generally on level ground. Due to stones having been removed for other purposes since then, the number of stones originally in each circle in this list is in most cases a well-informed guess.

Brisworthy, 98½in diameter, 40 stones
Buttern Hill, 97½in, 40
Fernworthy, 78¾in, 20
Grey Wethers (North), 126¾in, 30
Grey Wethers (South), 132¾in, 30
Langstone Moor, 82¾in, 16
Mardon Down, 150½in, 61
Merrivale, 74¾in, 20
Scorhill, 106¼in, 60
Sherberton, 116½in, unknown
Shoveldon, 69¾in, 13
Whit Moor, 79½in, 20

IRON AGE HILL FORTS

Hill forts are earthworks which were used as fortified refuges or defended settlements in the Bronze and Iron Ages, though a few were used after the Roman period. The fortification generally follows the contours of the hill, and consists of one or more lines of earthworks, with defensive walls or stockades, and external ditches. This list includes heights above sea level.

Beacon Castle, near Parracombe, overlooking the Heddon Valley, 950ft

Belbury Castle, near Ottery St Mary, 377ft

Berry Camp, near Branscombe, 459ft

Berry Castle, or Black Dog, near Crediton, 652ft

Berry Castle, Weare Gifford, near Torrington, 311ft

Berry Head, south-east of Brixham, partly destroyed by construction of fortifications during the Napoleonic Wars

Berry's Wood, near Newton Abbot, 246ft

Blackbury Camp, near Seaton, 607ft

Blackdown Rings, Loddiswell, near Kingsbridge, 607ft

Bolt Tail, headland, 196ft

Boringdon Camp, near Plympton, 459ft

Bremridge Wood, near South Molton, 574ft

Brent Hill, near South Brent, 1,020ft

Burley Wood, near Lydford, with a Norman motte-and-bailey nearby, 705ft

Burridge Fort, near Barnstaple, overlooking the Yeo and Bradiford rivers, 492ft

Cadbury Castle, near Bickleigh, overlooking the Exe Valley, used as site of camp by Parliamentarian forces during Civil War, 492ft

Capton, near Dartmouth, 606ft

Castle Close, near Stoodleigh, overlooking the River Exe, 682ft

Castle Dyke, near Chudleigh, 459ft

Castle Head, near Dunterton, Tavistock, overlooking the River Tamar, 328ft, with other, lower earthworks nearby

Castle Hill, two similarly named forts, one in Torrington, the site of the castle, the other a small earthwork south-east of the town overlooking the River Torridge

Clovelly Dykes, near Clovelly, covering about 20 acres, 688ft

Cotley Castle, near Dunchideock, 720ft

Cranbrook Castle, near Drewsteignton, overlooking the Teign Valley, 1,082ft

Cranmore Castle, near Tiverton, enclosing slopes from 390ft to 560ft

Cunnilear Camp, near Loxhore, Barnstaple, overlooking river Yeo, 360ft

Denbury Hill, near Newton Abbot, 524ft

Dewerstone, near Plympton, 210ft

Dolbury, Killerton Park, 419ft
Dumpdon Hill, Otter Valley, near Honiton, 800ft
Embury Beacon, near Clovelly, 492ft
Halwell Camp, near Totnes, 605ft
Hawkesdown Hill, near Axmouth, 433ft
Hembury, near Honiton, 583ft
Hembury Castle, Tyrhecott, near Buckland Brewer, 450ft
High Peak, on coast near Sidmouth, 515ft
Hillsborough, Ilfracombe, 377ft
Holbury, Holbeton, overlooking the Erme Estuary, 310ft
Holne Chase Castle, near Buckland-in-the-Moor, overlooking the
    River Dart 490ft
Huntsham Castle, near Tiverton, 850ft
Kentisbury Down, near Blackmore Gate, Exmoor, 1,050ft
Knowle Hill Castle, near Braunton, 295ft
Lee Wood, near Barnstaple, 390ft
Membury Castle, 670ft
Milber Down, near Newton Abbot, 360ft
Mockham Down, near Brayfordhill, Barnstaple, 1,015ft
Musbury Castle, near Axminster, 575ft
Myrtlebury, near Lynmouth, 490ft
Newberry Castle, near Combe Martin, 360ft
Noss, Dartmouth, overlooking Noss Point, Dartmouth Estuary,
    260ft
Peppercombe Castle, near Bucks Mills, Bideford, on cliffs partly
    lost to coastal erosion
Posbury, near Crediton, 590ft
Prestonbury Castle, near Cranbrook and Wooston Castles,
    overlooking the Teign Valley, 720ft
Raddon Top, near Shobrooke, Crediton, 770ft
Roborough Castle, near Lynton, 1,050ft
Seaton Down, Seaton, 410ft
Shoulsbury Castle, near Challacombe, Exmoor, 1,549ft
Sidbury Castle, overlooking the River Sid, 607ft
Slapton Castle, 213ft
Smythapark, near Bratton Fleming, 660ft
Stanborough, near Halwell, Totnes, 660ft
Stockland Great Castle, 690ft, and Stockland Little Castle, half a
    mile north-east, 575ft
Stoke Hill, near Exeter, 522ft

Voley Castle, near Parracombe, Lynton 755ft
Wasteberry Camp, near Plympton, 300ft
Wind Hill, near Lynmouth, 855ft
Windbury Head, near Clovelly, Hartland Peninsula, partly lost to
    coastal erosion, though some ramparts about 330ft still exist
Woodbury Castle, near Woodbury, Exeter, overlooking the Exe
    Estuary, 607ft
Woodbury, Norton Down, near Dartmouth, 475ft
Wooston Castle, overlooking Teign Valley, near Prestonbury and
    Cranbrook Castles, 655ft
Yarrowbury, near Bigbury, overlooking the Avon Estuary, 262ft
Yellowberries Copse, near South Brent, 508ft

DEVON'S ENVIRONMENTAL FIRST

In the spring of 2007, Modbury became the first town in Europe,
if not the world, to ban plastic bags. The campaign was launched
by BBC journalist Rebecca Hosking, after she had filmed a wildlife
programme in Hawaii and saw first-hand the damage caused to
wildlife and the environment by carelessly discarded bags. She
persuaded every shop in the town to stop giving them away,
and similar communities and businesses across the country soon
followed the town's example.

6

TRANSPORT

RAILWAYS

The earliest railway built in Devon was the Haytor Granite Railway, sometimes known as the Haytor Tramway. Built in 1820, its trucks were road wagons pulled by horsepower, and it carried granite from Haytor quarry to the basin of the Stover canal, from where it was taken by canal boat to Teignmouth. It closed in about 1858 at the same time as the quarry, as it was unable to compete with the cheaper Cornish granite.

The second, and in fact the first railway in the modern sense, was the Plymouth & Dartmoor Railway, the brainchild of Sir Thomas Tyrwhitt, former Private Secretary to the Prince of Wales and later MP for Plymouth. It was opened on 26 September 1823, and ran 23 miles from Sutton Pool to King Tor, near Princetown, with a 2-mile extension to the latter being completed soon afterwards.

The South Devon Railway Company built and operated a railway from Exeter to Plymouth and Torquay, with the first section being opened from Exeter to Teignmouth on 30 May 1846. It was extended to Newton Abbot later that year and to Totnes in May 1847, the route being completed when it reached Plymouth in April 1849. It was extended into Plymouth Great Western Docks a year later, and in 1853 opened a branch to Sutton Pool though converting part of the Plymouth & Dartmoor Railway to broad gauge. A branch was opened from Newton Abbot to Torquay in December 1848, was extended as the Dartmouth & Torbay Railway in August 1859, and reached Kingswear in August 1864.

Plymouth became a joint station when the Cornwall Railway opened in May 1859, as did the South Devon & Tavistock Railway a month later. The company was amalgamated with Great Western Railway on 1 February 1876. It was nationalised on 1 January 1948, and the former South Devon Railway became the responsibility of British Railways, Western Region.

The South Devon Railway Trust, a separate body altogether, is a charitable organisation which runs a heritage railway from Totnes to Buckfastleigh alongside the River Dart. It has its headquarters at Buckfastleigh, and is known as the South Devon Railway, formerly the Dart Valley Railway.

The North Devon Railway Company, originally planned as a feeder line to the Bristol & Exeter Railway, operated a line from

Cowley Bridge to Bideford, which later became part of the London & South Western Railway. Within a few years it had extended to give a rail connection to other towns in North Devon which previously relied on packhorse transport and coastal shipping. An Exeter to Barnstaple section followed the rivers Yeo and Taw. Several other smaller lines were gradually absorbed into the same company, including the Taw Vale Railway and Dock Company along the River Taw, the Exeter and Crediton Railway, the Bideford Extension Railway and the Torrington Extension Railway. In 1923 the L&SWR became part of the Southern Railway Company.

Stations – Exeter to Plymouth

Exeter St Davids	Bittaford Platform
Exeter St Thomas	Ivybridge
Exminster	Cornwood
Starcross	Plympton
Dawlish Warren	Laira Halt
Dawlish	Laira
Teignmouth	Lipson Vale Halt
Newton, later renamed	Mutley
Newton Abbot	Plymouth
Totnes	Plymouth Millbay
South Brent	
Wrangaton, later renamed	
Kingsbridge Road	

Stations – Torquay Branch
Kingskerswell
Torquay, later renamed Torre

Stations – Exeter & Crediton Railway
Cowley Bridge Junction
St Cyres, renamed Newton St Cyres in 1913
Crediton

Stations – North Devon Railway
Yeoford
Coleford Junction
Okehampton
Copplestone

Morchard Road
Lapford
Eggesford
South Molton Road
Portsmouth Arms
Umberleigh
Chapeltown, renamed Chapelton 1875
Barnstaple

Stations – Taw Vale Railway & Dock
Barnstaple
Fremington

Stations – Bideford Extension Railway
Instow
Bideford

Stations – L&SWR Torrington Extension
Bideford
Torrington

DISASTER!

Devon's worst railway tragedy was at Bere Ferrers station (on the former Southern main line between Exeter and Plymouth, via Okehampton) on 24 September 1917. A group of soldiers had just arrived in England from New Zealand and were being taken from Plymouth to Salisbury. At Bere Ferrers the train stopped, and they got out for a short break, but had assumed they would get out the same side of the carriage as they had entered. Tragically, the door they used took them straight into the path of an oncoming express. Nine were killed immediately and a tenth died in hospital shortly afterwards.

CANALS

The Grand Western Canal, from Taunton to Tiverton, was built to link the Bristol Channel and English Channel, but was never completed as planned as it was superseded by the advent of the railway. It was constructed in two parts, with one section from Tiverton to Lowdwells on the county border opened in 1814, and the Somerset section opened in 1839. The latter closed in 1867, with part of it having disappeared from the landscape and part still in use as a footpath. The Devon section closed in 1962 but was reopened in 1971, and is now known as the Tiverton Canal. Navigation is now restricted to unpowered boats, apart from a maintenance vessel used for cutting weed. The final section from Fossend to Lowdwells is a nature reserve. The whole waterway is a designated country park, with a horse-drawn tourist narrowboat running from Tiverton.

The Tavistock Canal, linking Tavistock to Morwellham Quay, River Tamar, where cargo could be loaded on to ships, was first used in 1805, completed in 1817 and closed in 1873, but is still used to supply water to a hydro-electric power plant at Morwellham.

Stover Canal, from Jetty Marsh, Newton Abbot, to Ventiford, built for the ball clay industry, was first used in 1792, and closed in 1937. It is now derelict although the Stover Canal Society has plans to restore it and reopen it for navigation.

Rolle (or Torrington) Canal, from Landcross where it joins the River Torridge, to the limekilns at Rosemoor, was completed in 1827 and closed in 1871.

Exeter Ship Canal, from Exeter to Topsham, was begun in about 1564 and is one of the oldest artificial waterways in England. Extended in 1677, it was last used commercially in 1972 and is now used for recreational purposes, mainly watersports.

Cann Quarry Canal, from Cann Quarry to the River Plym at Marsh Mills, was opened in 1829 but it had ceased to be used for navigation by about ten years later. The tracks of the Plymouth and Dartmoor Railway were laid along the canal bank, and part of it is still visible.

TRAMS

Plymouth's first street tramway, opened by the Plymouth, Stonehouse and Devonport Tramways Co. in 1872, ran from Derry's Clock along Union Street to Cumberland Gardens, Devonport. Although the network soon expanded, by 1941 the only line left was from Drake Circus to Peverell Corner. The final Plymouth tram journey was on 29 September 1945, when the last remaining vehicle started at Old Town Street and drove for the last time into the Milehouse depot.

Exeter ran a privately operated horse-drawn tramway from 1882 to 1905, when it was bought by the City Council who replaced the system with an electric tramway. Single-decker buses were introduced in 1929, and the last Exeter tram made its final journey on 15 August 1931.

Torquay Tramways Co. Ltd began a service around the town on 4 April 1907, and opened an extension connecting it with Paignton in July 1911. After a residents' poll, buses won the vote and the last Torquay tram ran on 31 January 1934.

The Seaton Tramway, 3 miles long and running along the Axe Valley from Seaton to Colyton, was established in 1950. Operated by Modern Electric Tramways, it was originally built as a hobby by an enthusiast who made electric milk floats for a living and decided to build a large-scale model tram to exhibit and run at local resorts, where it attracted so much attention that he expanded it into a regular venture. Parts of the track run on the bed of the old British Rail Seaton line.

TURNPIKE TRUSTS

Until the end of the nineteenth century, highway maintenance was the responsibility of individual parishes. With growth of manufacturing industry and the need to transport raw materials and finished goods, increasing traffic required a new means of dealing with the maintenance of roads, which led to an Act of Parliament in the eighteenth century sanctioning the formation of turnpike trusts. These were permitted to build roads and charge tolls. The following trusts were established in Devon.

Stonehouse, 1751, 4 miles (later absorbed into Plymouth Eastern)
Exeter, 1753, 141 miles
Axminster, 1754, 22 miles
Honiton, 1754, 51 miles
Ashburton & Totnes, 1755, 25 miles
Plymouth Eastern, 1758, 15 miles
Tiverton, 1759, 86 miles
Kingsbridge & Dartmouth, 1759, 63 miles
Modbury, 1759, 16 miles
South Molton, 1759, 76 miles
Great Torrington, 1759, 71 miles
Okehampton, 1760, 43 miles
Saltash, 1762, 8 miles (included some Plymouth roads)
Tavistock, 1762, 51 miles
Totnes & Berry Pomeroy, 1762, 44 miles
Barnstaple, 1763, 104 miles
Bideford, 1764, 49 miles
Newton Bushel (Abbot), 1765, 24 miles
Torquay & Dartmouth, 1765, 44 miles
Countess Wear Bridge, 1769, 2 miles
Moretonhampstead, 1772, 13 miles

Honiton & Ilminster, 1807, 12 miles
Plymouth & Tavistock, 1812, 16 miles
Cullompton, 1813, 6 miles
Honiton & Sidmouth, 1816, 7 miles
Plymouth & Exeter Road, 1822, 5 miles
Teignmouth & Dawlish, 1823, 24 miles
Braunton, 1829, 5 miles
Exmouth, 1832, 2 miles
Combe Martin, 1838, 22 miles
Braunton & Ilfracombe, 1843, 10 miles
Sidmouth & Cullompton, 1846, 16 miles

DEVON'S MAJOR ROADS

The A30 runs from Staines, near London, to Land's End, a distance
of 284 miles, and it was known as the Great South West Road.
It was the most direct route until superseded by the M3 and the
A303, and has trunk road status between Honiton and Penzance,
where it is mostly dual carriageway although it has some sections
of single carriageway. As well as Honiton, it also passes through
Exeter, and bypasses Okehampton.

The A39 runs from Bath, through Somerset, North Devon,
Exmoor, to the South Cornwall coast, a distance of 204 miles. The
section from the North Devon Link Road at Barnstaple to the A30
at Fraddon, Cornwall, is known as the Atlantic Highway.

The A361 runs from Ilfracombe to Barnstaple, along the North
Devon coast, hence its name the North Devon Link Road, to
Tiverton, then to Taunton and terminates at a junction on the
Northamptonshire–Warwickshire border. Covering a distance of
195 miles, it is the longest three-digit A road in Britain.

The A38 runs from Bodmin, Cornwall, to Mansfield,
Nottinghamshire, a distance of 292 miles. Until the M5 was
opened, it was the main South-West holiday route. The 42-mile
stretch from Exeter to Plymouth is also known as the Devon
Expressway. The M5, which begins at a junction with the M6 near
West Bromwich and ends at Exeter, reached Devon in 1969.

DEVON'S ROAD ACCIDENTS

According to official figures from Devon County Council, in 2009 Teignmouth had the highest number of road accidents in Devon during the previous four years. In 2008 there were 9 fatal accidents, 47 serious crashes and 498 minor collisions. In the same period East Devon also had 9 fatal accidents, 37 serious crashes and 462 minor collisions, and South Hams 3 fatal accidents, 35 serious crashes and 352 minor collisions. The main cause of accidents was speeding, leading local councillors to campaign for a reduction in the speed limit on specific roads.

In 2001, Devon reported 3,367 injuries as a result of road accidents, of which 375 were serious cases, and 46 fatalities. The worst months for these were January and October.

SHIPWRECKS

There have been several hundred shipwrecks off the Devon coasts, and this list gives only a selection in chronological order, including some of those with the worst fatalities. The date of wreckage follows the name of the vessel.

Arms of Bristol, 26 March 1675, 350 tons, sailing from Bristol to Barbados, wrecked off Ilfracombe with the loss of 16, although 40 reached land.

HMS *Coronation*, 3 September 1691, 90-gun ship of the line, sunk in a storm off Rame Head with about 600 lost and only 20 survivors.

HMS *Ramillies*, 14 February 1760, 1,700-ton, 90-gun ship of the line, originally built as HMS *Royal Katherine* in 1664, later refitted, expanded and renamed in honour of John Churchill's victory at the battle of Ramillies in 1706 during the War of the Spanish Succession. In almost continuous service for over ninety years, she was wrecked off Bolt Head in what would remain the greatest maritime tragedy in South-West waters for many years. Exact figures are uncertain, but it is thought that of a total crew of about 850, only about 20 survived.

HMS *Weasel*, 12 January 1799, sank off Baggy Point, Croyde Bay, with loss of 106, and the purser the only survivor.

Betsey, 3 March 1831, a sloop sailing from Wales to Barnstaple, capsized in Barnstaple Bay with the loss of three men.

Thomas Crisp, 18 January 1850, schooner sailing from Bristol to Barbados, struck Morte Stone off the North Devon coast near Woolacombe, with one man lost.

Soudan, 27 June 1887, 844-ton French steamer, sailing from Senegal, wrecked off Hamstone, near Salcombe.

SS *Nepaul*, 10 December 1890, 3,536 tons, owned by P&O Steam Navigation Co., wrecked off Plymouth between Shag Stone and the Mew Stone.

HMS *Formidable*, 1 January 1915, battleship carrying out exercises in English Channel, sunk after being hit by two torpedoes from a German submarine in rough seas near Berry Head, with the loss of 35 officers and 512 men out of a total complement of 780.

HMS *Foyle*, 15 March 1917, hit a mine near Dover and 27 crew out of 70 were killed. She was towed to Plymouth, but was too badly damaged to make the complete journey, and sank off the Mew Stone.

Yvonne, 3 September 1920, 4-masted barquetine, sailing from Jamaica for France, wrecked at Plymouth Breakwater, with the loss of the ship's cook.

Herzogin Cecilie, 25 January 1936, German four-mast barque or windjammer, given to France as part of reparation after the First World War and sold to a Finnish owner, but while sailing from Falmouth to Ipswich, struck the Hamstone, just off the coast at Salcombe.

SS *Louis Sheid*, 7 December 1939, 6,057-ton Belgian steamer, ran aground off the coast near Kingsbridge.

SUBMARINE DISASTERS

Submarine *A8*, 8 June 1905, lost outside Plymouth Breakwater while on routine training exercises when tons of water came through a faulty hatch seal and she exploded underwater – 15 men were killed and four rescued.

USS *Minneapolis-St Paul*, 29 December 2006, four men fell overboard while working on routine maintenance on vessel in Plymouth Sound. Two died and two were rescued.

DEVON LIGHTHOUSES

All are active unless otherwise stated

Berry Head, Brixham – England's smallest lighthouse
Braunton Sands Low, Crown Point
Brixham Breakwater
Dartmouth Castle (inactive since about 1886)

Eddystone
Exmouth Customs House
Hartland Point
Ilfracombe, Lantern Hill
Kingswear
Lundy Island Beacon Hill (inactive since 1897 and replaced by
   the two below)
Lundy Island North
Lundy Island South
Lynmouth Foreland
Mortehoe, Bull Point
Plymouth Breakwater
Plymouth Ocean Court, Hamoaze
Plymouth, Queen Anne's Battery
Shaldon
Start Point
Teignmouth

There have been four Eddystone lighthouses off Rame Head, the first one being lit in 1698, destroyed in a storm in 1703. The second, completed in 1709, was destroyed in 1755. Smeaton's Tower, completed in 1759, remained in use until 1877 when it was deemed unsafe because of erosion of the rocks, rebuilt on Plymouth Hoe and was replaced by a newer lighthouse on Eddystone Rocks.

The original Kingswear lighthouse on the cliff was demolished in 1980 as it had become unsafe, and was replaced by a new one in 1981.

AIRPORTS

Plymouth City Airport, opened July 1931, 3,809ft long – due to close December 2011

Exeter International Airport, opened July 1938, 6,833ft long

AIR CRASHES

Dartmoor, Hameldon Tor, 21 March 1941, four crew killed when an aeroplane from 49 Squadron from Bomber Command crashed in poor visibility.

Dartmoor, near Okehampton, 22 August 1941, one died, three taken prisoner when an aeroplane from 152 Squadron was shot down by a Spitfire while on a reconnaissance mission over Filton, Bristol.

Dartmoor, Tiger's Marsh, near Black Tor Copse, 25 December 1943, five killed and another three injured when 8th Air Force B17 crashed in poor visibility.

FOOD & DRINK

FOOD

Devonshire cream tea, consisting of scones, jam and clotted cream, is said to have originated in Devon, though other counties have made similar claims. In Australia, New Zealand and other countries, it is known as 'Devonshire tea'.

White pudding is known as Hog's pudding in Devon and Cornwall.

Devonshire Quarrendon apples, an old deep crimson variety of fruit, were first recorded in about 1680. They are an unusual variety with a distinct strawberry flavour, regarded as best when eaten fresh from the tree. The best picking time is late August.

Devon produces over 30 different varieties of cheese, and the county's largest cheese producer is the Taw Valley Creamery, supplied by a number of dairy farms. Among Devon cheeses are Curworthy, Sharpham, Tickler, Vulscombe, Devon Blue and Beenleigh Blue.

Devon cattle are rich red in colour, and sometimes known as Devon Ruby or Red Ruby. They are also sometimes known as North Devon, to avoid confusion with South Devon cattle. Sometimes called Orange Elephants, they are the largest of the British native breeds, and are thought to have descended from the large red cattle of Normandy, brought over at the time of the Norman Conquest. Although used mostly for beef, they are on occasion farmed for milking as well.

Riverford Farm, near Buckfastleigh, is the county's most famous vegetable supplier. It began when founder Guy Watson started delivering locally to 30 friends in Devon, and grew to a national business delivering 47,000 boxes a week to homes around the United Kingdom from regional sister farms in Peterborough, Hampshire, Yorkshire and Cheshire. The group has 230 employees, 60,000 customers, an annual turnover of £33 million, and 70 per cent of their produce is grown in Great Britain. They won the Best Online Retailer 2010 award at the Observer Ethical Awards.

The Ambrosia company, Lifton, founded in 1917 as an infant nutrition company and now owned by Premier Foods, was the first in Britain to produce tinned rice pudding and custard. The rice pudding, made from local milk, was always used in Red Cross food parcels.

F.H. Jacka, the Barbican, Plymouth, is Britain's oldest commercial bakery, founded by the Fownes family in 1596. During the blitz, local families came here to cook their dinners in the coal-fired ovens when power supplies were interrupted by bombing raids.

DRINK

The Plymouth Gin Distillery, sometimes known locally as the Blackfriars Distillery, Southside Street, has been producing gin since 1793. It was known as Coates & Co. until 2004, after which it was bought by the Swedish company V&S Group, and since 2008 it

has been owned and distributed by the French company Pernod Ricard. It was a favourite drink of Winston Churchill, Alfred Hitchcock, Franklin D. Roosevelt and Ian Fleming, among others.

Devon is home to several breweries including:

Beer Engine, Newton St Cyres, Exeter
Blewitt's Brewery, Kingsbridge
Branscombe Vale, Branscombe
Clearwater Brewery, Torrington
Dartmoor Brewery, Princetown – the highest in England
Jolly Boat Brewery, Bideford
Otter Brewery, Luppitt, near Honiton
Teignworthy Brewery, Newton Abbot

The Heavitree Brewery, based at Heavitree, Exeter, was established in about 1790. It was the last brewery in Exeter to cease production, continuing until 1970, and the buildings were demolished in 1980. The name survives as the owner of a chain of pubs in the West Country, and Heavitree Brewery PLC still exists as a quoted company with an address in Exeter. At the end of the nineteenth century there were fifteen breweries in the city – how times change!

Thomas Ford & Son's Brewery was established at Tiverton in 1852. It was acquired by Starkey, Knight & Co., Bridgwater, in 1895, becoming Starkey, Knight & Ford, and the same company also took over the Taw Vale Brewery, Barnstaple, in 1897. In 1962 the company became part of Whitbread.

Beverage Brands, based in Torquay, the producers of WKD Original Vodka, cider and various soft drink brands, was founded in 1992. It claims to be 'the No. 1 manufacturer of RTD (Ready To Drink) brands in Britain'.

PUBS WITH LITERARY CONNECTIONS

Burgh Island Hotel, Burgh Island – a favourite Devon stopping-place of Noel Coward, Winston Churchill, Amy Johnson and, so it is said, Edward VIII and Mrs Simpson, as well as Agatha Christie, who based the Jolly Roger Inn in *Evil Under the Sun* on it.

George Hotel, South Molton – R.D. Blackmore mentions it by name in *Lorna Doone*.

Journey's End, Ringmore – R.C. Sherriff wrote much of his play of the same name, first performed in 1929, there.

Manor House Hotel, Moretonhampstead – Evelyn Waugh wrote much of *Put Out More Flags* while staying there.

Pack'o'Cards, Combe Martin – Marie Corelli stayed there, probably while writing *The Mighty Atom*, which was set in nearby Clovelly.

Rock Inn, Georgeham – a favourite haunt of Henry Williamson, who visited regularly and gathered a certain amount of material for his novels while chatting to friends and patrons. Drawings and photos of him are still displayed on the walls.

Royal Hotel, Bideford – Charles Kingsley stayed in this former merchant's house in 1854, and probably wrote part of *Westward Ho!* (1855) there.

Royal Hotel, Dartmouth – disguised as the Royal George in Agatha Christie's *Ordeal by Innocence*.

Royal Seven Stars, Totnes – Daniel Defoe alludes to it in his book, *A Tour Through the Whole Island of Great Britain* (1724) (see also pp. 46–7).

Three Crowns Inn, Chagford – Sidney Godolphin, one of the Cavalier Poets and staunch supporter of Charles I, was ambushed in the town by Parliamentarian forces, attacked and carried into the porch where he died of his wounds.

OTHER PUBS, HOTELS & RESTAURANTS WITH INTERESTING ASSOCIATIONS

The Stag Inn, Rackenford, near Tiverton, dates back to the end of the twelfth century and is believed to be Devon's oldest remaining pub.

The Drewe Arms, Drewsteignton, was originally called the Druid Arms, until the Drewe family at Castle Drogo, who were having Castle Drogo built nearby, persuaded the brewery to change the name. It was taken over in 1919 by Ernest and Mabel Mudge, who had married in 1916. After Ernest died in 1951 his widow continued to run it herself, finally retiring on 4 October 1994, her ninety-ninth birthday, the oldest and the longest-serving landlady in Britain at the time. She died two years later.

The Royal Clarence Hotel, Exeter, built by William Mackworth Praed in 1769 as the Assembly Rooms, is recognised as the first hotel in England. An advertisement using the word 'hotel' (from the French for hostel) was published by the first landlord, the Frenchman Pierre Berlon, in September 1770. It was successively and unofficially known as the Cadogen Hotel, the Phillips Hotel, Thompsons, or simply 'the Hotel', until 1827, when the name was officially changed in honour of the Duchess of Clarence, later Queen Adelaide, who stayed there.

The China House, Plymouth, overlooking the Barbican and Sutton Harbour, was originally a warehouse built probably in the seventeenth century, believed to have been used for storage by William Cookworthy, 'the father of English porcelain'. It has also been used as a gun wharf and a hospital for mariners.

The Exeter Inn, Modbury, was bought and owned in the 1980s by Graham Knight, bass guitarist with and founder member of pop-rock group Marmalade, who remained with them from their formation in the 1960s until 2010.

11 The Quay, Ilfracombe, is a quayside seafood restaurant and bar owned by controversial artist Damien Hirst. Despite what one of his previous artistic creations might lead one to expect, shark in formaldehyde has never been on the menu.

The Maltsters Arms, Tuckenhay, near Totnes, was bought in 1989 by Keith Floyd (1943–2009), the well-known TV chef. He renamed it Floyd's Inn (Sometimes) and ran it for seven years until going bankrupt, apparently after a £36,000 cheque for a drinks bill bounced.

The Highwayman Inn, Sourton, built in about 1280, was given its present name in 1959 when John Buster Jones and his wife Rita brought the then run-down property and transformed it. It prides itself on its decor, which is said to rank among the most unusual of any pub in the county. The entrance has been built to resemble an old Launceston to Tavistock coach, and in the Locker bar, the main surface is a huge piece of wood brought from a Dartmoor bog. Many of the fittings have been created to look like the bows of an old wooden ship, with old timbers from vessels, notably the carved door of a whaling ship, *Diana*, which ran aground in the Humber in 1869.

The Valiant Soldier, Buckfastleigh, is 'the pub where time was never called'. When the last landlady gave up her licence in 1965, it was left exactly as it was when it closed, with furniture and fittings left intact, and nothing packed up or thrown away. It stood untouched until 1997, when it was acquired by Teignbridge District Council, who now run it as a museum and heritage centre in association with the local community.

Veggie Perrin, Mayflower Street, Plymouth, a cruelty-free restaurant ('no fish, prawns or even eggs') took its name, almost, from the central character in the BBC television comedy series *The Fall and Rise of Reginald Perrin*. Leonard Rossiter, who had played the title role, was long since dead, and the opening ceremony was performed by his co-star, actor John Barron, who played the eccentric office boss CJ. The restaurant's strapline, 'I didn't get where I am today by eating meat', took its cue from CJ's catchphrase in the series.

WHAT'S IN A (PUB) NAME?

Here are some local hostelries, not all still in existence, with interesting names and obvious, or not so obvious, reasons why and how they acquired them.

Blue Monkey, Plymouth
Previously known variously as Church Inn, St Bude Inn, St Budeaux Inn, and even Ye Old St Budeaux Inn, its name was changed in about 1939. Some say that it was because somebody had seen a monkey climbing on the roof, others that it was in honour of the boys who packed the guns with powder at the Battle of Trafalgar and were left with a blue residue on their hands. Towards the end of its days it developed a bad reputation, closed and was put on the market, but failed to sell. It was partly destroyed in an arson attack, and in 2007 the remains were demolished.

Brown Bear, Plymouth
Opened in 1774 as The Bear, adding Brown a few years later, as it had a large bear pit in the cellar used for fights before the practice

was outlawed. It later changed its name briefly to the Chapel Street Inn but has since reverted.

Clarence Hotel, Plymouth
Named after the Duke of Clarence, who as Prince William had occasionally visited the city.

Elephant's Nest, Horndon, near Mary Tavy
Formerly the New Inn (and who could resist changing from a dull name like that), it was changed in 1952 after the customers good-naturedly teased the overweight landlord, telling him he looked like an elephant on his nest. He evidently took it in good spirits.

Falstaff Inn, Plymouth
Named after the renowned bon viveur Sir John Falstaff of Shakespeare's plays.

Grand Duchess, Plymouth; The Oldenburg, Paignton
Both named after Marie, Grand Duchess of Oldenburg, who had visited Devon on occasion.

Northmore Arms, Wonson, near Whiddon Dow
Another which could not wait to get rid of a boring New Inn appellation, altering it in the 1970s in hour of Mr Northmore, who had lived in Manor House at Wonson, until he was careless enough to lose his estate on the turn of a card. He gambled on his estate and lost, beaten by the ace of diamonds.

Pack Horse, South Brent
A former pack horse station on the old Plymouth to London turnpike road.

Palk Arms, Hennock
Named after the Palks who were landowners in the area.

Plume of Feathers, Princetown
Named after the three ostrich feathers from the arms of the Prince of Wales. Formerly called the Prince's Arms, Princetown's oldest building was originally erected to house the workmen engaged to build the town.

8

INDUSTRY & POPULATION

MINING

Tin mining in Devon began in Roman times, mostly on Dartmoor. In the eighteenth century the area was the major European source of the metal. Stannary towns included Plympton, Chagford, Tavistock and Ashburton. The county's stannary department met at Crockern Tor, Dartmoor.

In Victorian times, after the discovery of a copper lode at Morwellham in 1844, Devon Great Consols (DGC), near Tavistock, including the mines of Wheal Maria, Wheal Fanny, Wheal Anna Maria, Wheal Josiah, Wheal Emma, Wheal Frementor, Watson's Mine and Frementor, was the largest copper mine in the world. Production of copper reached a peak in 1862, with 41,513 tons produced. The area was also rich in arsenic and lead. By the end of the century deposits were exhausted, and DGC closed in May 1901.

In Hemerdon tungsten and tin were discovered in 1867, but it was last worked in 1944, though in 2007 plans were announced to reopen the mine. The last iron mine worked in Devon was Great Rock Mine, near Bovey Tracey, which closed in 1969, and the last remaining grante quarry, at Merrivale, closed in 1997.

LOCAL POTTERY

The Aller Vale Pottery was founded in 1865 in the hamlet of Aller, near Kingskerswell. It was taken over in 1868 by John Phillips (1835–97), a clay merchant from Newton Abbot, and after a period specialising in builders' earthenware, including drainpipes, chimney pots and roof tiles, it began producing art pottery in 1881 when it was renamed the Aller Vale Art Pottery. After Phillips died, it was acquired by Hexter Humpherson & Co., who amalgamated it with another company they had recently acquired, Watcombe

Pottery, to form Royal Aller Vale & Watcombe Co. Simplified to 'Royal Watcombe', it continued making mottoware for the tourist market until it closed in 1962.

Honiton earthenware pottery, mainly Jacobean in design, established in 1918, was largely the work of Charles Collard, who had formerly worked at the Aller Vale Pottery, Kingskerswell, and at the Crown Dorset Art Pottery, Poole. The company had its heyday in the 1930s, with Collard's daughter Joan as the chief decorator and host to visitors who called in at the works. He retired due partly to failing eyesight in 1947 and sold the company. It ceased trading in 1997 and the name was sold to Dartmouth Pottery, established in 1947.

PHILATELY

The internationally famous firm specialising in what was for a long time regarded as the most popular hobby of all, Stanley Gibbons Ltd, had its origins in Plymouth. Stanley Gibbons (1840–1913) began selling postage stamps to collectors from a desk in the corner of his father's pharmacy. When his father died in 1867 he took over the business, trading as a chemist and stamp dealer, selling the pharmaceutical side and relocating to larger premises in 1872, moving to London two years later. Married five times, he outlived four of his wives, leaving no children, and it is said that although still married to the fifth Mrs Gibbons, he died in the arms of a mistress at the Savoy Hotel, and to avoid scandal his body was concealed in a carpet and quietly removed to his nephew's home nearby. The premature deaths of his first four wives has led to speculation that his training in the family business of chemistry may have enabled him to become a secret serial killer.

POPULATION

In Elizabethan times, Devon was said to be the second most populous county in England, after Yorkshire. After the census was introduced, records showed that between 1801 and 1831 she was fourth in the table, but had fallen to ninth by 1881, and fifteenth by 1951.

DEVON'S TOP 20 CITIES & TOWNS BY POPULATION

Figures taken from the 2001 census returns.

1.	Plymouth	240,720
2.	Exeter	111,076
3.	Torquay	63,998
4.	Paignton	48,251
5.	Exmouth	32,972
6.	Newton Abbot	23,550
7.	Barnstaple	20,724
8.	Tiverton	18,621
9.	Brixham	17,457
10.	Teignmouth	14,413
11.	Bideford	14,407
11.	Sidmouth	14,407
13.	Dawlish	13,135
14.	Ivybridge	12,056
15.	Northam	11,604
16.	Tavistock	11,018
17.	Honiton	10,857
18.	Ilfracombe	10,840
19.	Kingsteignton	10,615
20.	Cullompton	7,609

DEVON'S MEDIEVAL TOP FIVE

According to a survey of 1523 of all laypersons whose real estate amounted to £40 per year or more, the following were the wealthiest towns in Devon.

1. Exeter
2. Totnes
3. Plymouth
4. Colyton
5. Tavistock

PLYMOUTH'S POPULATION
THROUGH THE AGES

In 1377, the Subsidy Roll of laypersons aged fourteen and over in Plymouth who were eligible to pay the poll tax was 4,837, suggesting a total population of about 7,000. Roughly the same figure is estimated for around 1600, the lack of increase being ascribed to the prevalence of disease and also frequent attacks by the French, which led some people to move inland. In 1733, the number of people in Plymouth Dock (which became Devonport in 1824) was estimated at 3,361, and in Plymouth 8,400.

The following figures are taken from the census returns for Plymouth. Up to and including 1911 there were separate figures for each of the three towns, Plymouth, Devonport and Stonehouse. Between 1801 and 1831 Devonport was the most populous of all three, with this position being reversed from 1841 onwards, and Stonehouse always being the smallest by a considerable margin. Owing to the Second World War there was no 1941 census, and as the 1951 figure shows, the figure had fallen substantially as a result of the exodus from the city during wartime and many not returning in peacetime.

1921	210,036
1931	227,631
1951	208,985
1961	231,505
1971	239,452
1981	243,895
1991	243,373
2001	240,720

At the time of writing, the latest figure available (November 2010) is 256,700, showing a significant increase on the falls since 1981.

EXETER'S POPULATION
THROUGH THE AGES

1801	17,412
1811	18,896
1821	23,479
1831	28,242
1841	30,712
1851	32,823
1861	33,738
1871	34,650
1881	37,665
1891	37,404
1901	47,185
1911	48,664
1921	59,582
1931	67,607
1951	75,513
1961	88,598
1971	99,515
1981	95,621
1991	98,125
2001	111,078

9

WAR, RELIGION &
FOLKLORE

RELIGION IN DEVON

Christianity was introduced to Devon in the first century AD. Many Cornish saints are also commemorated in Devon in legends, churches and place-names. The most notable of these is St Petroc, who is said to have passed through Devon – the villages of Petrockstowe and Newton St Petroc are named after him, and the Devon flag is also dedicated to him. The following Devon towns and villages have churches named after him:

Ashburton (Our Lady of Lourdes and St Petroc)
Dartmouth
Harford
Inwardleigh, Exeter
Ivybridge
Lydford
Parracombe
Petton, Bampton
South Brent

The other main Devon saint is St Boniface, also sometimes called Winfrid, Wynfrith, or Wynfryth, probably at Crediton, a missionary who went to spread Christianity in the Frankish Empire during the seventh century, and was killed in AD 754. He is the patron saint of Germany, and of tailors and brewers. His national shrine in Britain is at the Roman Catholic Church of St Boniface at Crediton, and there was formerly a church dedicated to St Boniface at St Budeaux, Plymouth, now demolished. The

Roman Catholic Bishop of Plymouth, George Errington, founded St Boniface's Catholic College in Wyndham Square, Plymouth in 1856.

St Urith, St Hieritha, or St Iwerydd, was born at East Stowford, near Barnstaple, in the seventh or eighth century. A fervent Christian, she founded a church at Chittlehampton, and was said to have been attacked and beheaded by a group of local female haymakers, or alternatively killed by an invading Saxon or Viking force. A stream and flowers immediately appeared at the point where she was cut down. She was buried at Chittlehampton church, where people would travel from some distance to come and visit her shrine. Each year on her feast day, 8 July, local children take part in a procession to bless her holy well and lay bunches of flowers at the church in her memory.

In 1549 the Act of Uniformity introduced the Protestant Book of Common Prayer, making the old Latin service books illegal. The new book was bitterly resented by many, and when Father Harper, Vicar of St Andrew's Church, Sampford Courtenay, used it on Whit Sunday his parishioners demanded that he should revert to using the old one. At the next service, magistrates were present to ensure that this did not happen. A scuffle arose and when William Helyons, a local farmer and outspoken supporter of the new book, quarrelled with others on the steps of the church house, one picked up a pitchfork, ran it through him and left him dead. A group of parishioners marched to Exeter and besieged the city on 2 July in what became known as the Prayer Book Rebellion, demanding the withdrawal of all English scriptures. The city kept its gates closed for over a month, and Sir Gawain Carew, a Privy Councillor, and Lord John Russell, 1st Earl of Bedford, were sent to put down the revolt. There were skirmishes between the rebels and government troops at Fenny Bridges, Clyst Heath and Sampford Courtenay, in which the former were defeated. The survivors fled, but most were rounded up and executed. Over 5,000, on both sides, were killed as a result of the rebellion.

The Exeter diocese, including the whole of Devon, remains the Anglican diocese. A Roman Catholic diocese was established at Plymouth in the mid-nineteenth century.

Devon has two of Britain's oldest synagogues. One is at Catherine Street, Plymouth, built in 1762, and the other at Mary Arches Street, Exeter, built a year later.

OTHER DEVON CHURCHES

Most of Devon's most interesting and picturesque churches inevitably date from the fourteenth and fifteenth centuries, considered the golden age of ecclesiastical craftsmanship, and occasionally earlier.

Ashton, Church of St John the Baptist, near Chudleigh
Fifteenth-century church noted for its interior and fourteenth-century panels, which have retained their original colours, and a particularly fine Elizabethan pulpit. The turret stair leading to the rood loft can still be climbed.

Atherington, Church of St Mary, near Barnstaple
Perpendicular church restored in 1884, with a screen and gallery dating back to probably the fifteenth century. The north aisle part of the screen, carved by two Chittlehampton craftsmen in about 1540, retains its original canopy. Elizabethan heraldic panels are preserved in the loft.

Holy Trinity Church, Burrington, near Barnstaple
Church built between 1150 and 1550 by the Abbot of Tavistock Abbey and cared for by Benedictine monks until the Dissolution of the Monasteries, and extensively restored in 1869. It has an old granite arcade, wagon roof with carved bosses, an early sixteenth-century rood screen and a Norman font. Samuel Davis, whose second wife Jane Blackmore was the half-sister of R.D. Blackmore of *Lorna Doone* fame, was vicar during the nineteenth century.

St Hieritha's Church, Chittlehampton, Umberleigh
This church of the late Perpendicular period is the site of the healing well and shrine of St Urith, or Hieritha (see p. 141), who is believed to have been buried underneath, in the small chapel on the north side of the sanctuary. The 115ft tower is considered the

finest in Devon. The pulpit, carved in about 1500, shows St Urith holding a martyr's palm and the foundation stone of the church.

Church of St Mary Magdalene, Chulmleigh

This church, rebuilt in the fifteenth century, has an 86ft tower. The interior is decorated with a sixteenth-century rood screen, surmounted by wooden figures of the four evangelists.

St Andrew's Church, Cullompton

With its striking red sandstone tower 100ft tall and pinnacles on top, built in about 1545, it is regarded as one of the most striking churches in Devon. The interior has a boarded wagon roof in blue, crimson and gold, stretching the whole length of the building. The west has damaged remains of a crucifixion scene with figures of King Edward VI and St George on either side. At the rear is the 'Golgotha' or Calvary, two large pieces of oak, once the base of a rood screen, carved with skulls, rocks and bones, to remind worshippers of the short span of life on earth, probably removed from the church in 1549 and cut in two but later rescued.

St Saviour's Church, Dartmouth

A fourteenth-century church remarkable for its wood carving, especially on the rood screen, dating from 1480. The west gallery is embellished with the coats of arms of important local families, including Hawkins and Drake, painted in 1633. The south door, decorated with two Plantagenet leopards, is thought to be the original from 1372.

All Saints, East Budleigh

Another church with a red sandstone tower, its most remarkable connections are those of the Raleigh family. The bench ends, believed to be among the oldest surviving ones in England, are about 500 years old, and include the Raleigh pew with the family coat of arms. Sir Walter's father was one of the churchwardens, and his second wife is buried in the centre aisle, the place marked by a floriated cross and surrounded by a Latin inscription cut in reverse, thought to be the result of a craftsman reading a tracing the wrong way round.

Church of St George, George Nympton, near South Molton

This church has no street frontage, being entered along a path through a garden gate between two thatched cottages. The original tower was destroyed by fire and rebuilt in 1673 with bricks made in a nearby field. The organ, one of twenty-five made in the Queen Anne period, is a four-octave single manual pipe instrument on which the black and white keys have their colours reversed.

St Mary's Church, High Bickington, near Barnstaple

This twelfth-century church was enlarged with the addition of the north aisle and a south tower, making it the only church in the county with two towers. The Norman font, decorated with Maltese crosses and chevrons, was restored at one stage but fell into pieces when the encircling iron bands holding it together were removed, and had to be painstakingly reassembled.

St Mary's Church, Honeychurch, near Okehampton

The original church is twelfth-century, with a west tower and south porch added in the fifteenth century. It is considered one of the smallest, most unsophisticated in the county. The tower has three medieval bells in their original cage, the Norman font a Jacobean cover, and the late medieval benches are mostly of plain unvarnished oak.

All Saints, Kenton

The fourteenth-century red sandstone church, with its 100ft tower, has carved heads on the porch thought to represent Henry IV and Queen Joan. The white Beer stone arcades are carved with foliage and various sculpted figures, and the fifteenth-century rood screen is considered one of the finest in the county. The pulpit, hewn from a large oak tree, was thrown away at some period but later rescued and restored in the nineteenth century.

St James's Church, Kings Nympton

Mostly fifteenth-century, the west tower is probably older. All the roofs, including that of the porch, have carved bosses portraying foliage and heads of men and women, and there is an eighteenth-century painted ceiling above the chancel. The granite step to the porch is a former Celtic cross.

St Mary's Church, Molland, near Barnstaple

This Perpendicular church is notable for its well-preserved Georgian interior. It has a memorial to the Revd O. Barry, who was persecuted for his adherence to the Royalist cause during the Civil War. The west face has two large tablets bearing the Ten Commandments and a panel between the royal arms, and in the north aisle is a three-decker pulpit with canopy.

St Mary's, Ottery St Mary

Sometimes referred to as a miniature replica of Exeter Cathedral, 164ft long, it is renowned for its painted roof and fan-vaulted aisle. The south transept, or bell tower, contains an astronomical clock, one of the oldest surviving mechanical clocks in the country, attributed to Bishop John de Grandisson, Bishop of Exeter 1327–69. There are ten misericords, five showing the arms of the Bishop.

St Petroc's Church, Parracombe

The church was probably built in the late eleventh century by William of Falaise, a close relation of William the Conqueror, with the tower being added in 1182 and the chancel in 1252. Much of the current fabric dates from sixteenth-century reconstruction. Fears about its stability in 1879 resulted in the building of a new church in the village, Christ Church. Protests about the threatened demolition of St Petroc's, led by John Ruskin, resulted in its being retained as a mortuary chapel. The bells were removed and transferred to the new church. It was declared redundant in 1969 and two years later became the first to be vested in the Churches Conservation Trust.

St Andrew's Church, Plymouth

Begun in the eleventh century, it underwent regular enlargement over the next three centuries or so. It is the largest parish church in the county at 184ft long and with a tower 136ft tall. It was extensively restored by Sir George Gilbert Scott in the Victorian era, and largely destroyed during the Second World War, with only the walls and tower left standing. The rebuilt structure was reconsecrated in 1957. The new organ is the largest church organ west of Bristol.

St Petroc's Church, South Brent

The Norman tower of this church was the central tower of a cruciform building, of which the west portion was demolished probably in the early fourteenth century when the existing nave was rebuilt with two transepts, later enlarged into aisles. The partly fifteenth-century manor house is to the south of the churchyard. In 1436 the vicar, the Revd John Hay, was dragged out of the church while officiating at divine service and murdered, and the door through which he was taken has been walled up, the old doorway still being just visible.

St Andrew's Church, South Tawton

The fifteenth-century church, built mostly of granite and stone from Beer, has a striking series of carved angels attached to the wall plates and several figures carved on the bosses of the nave, chancel and aisle roofs. Beneath the lychgate is a stone coffin table with a stone stile by its side.

St Peter's Church, Tawstock

The fourteenth-century church is noted particularly for its collection of monuments, commemorating mostly members of the family of the Earls of Bath, and two ceilings of Italian plasterwork.

Holy Trinity Church, Torbryan

A fifteenth-century church with a Perpendicular three-stage tower and a medieval carved rood screen with panels showing paintings of saints and stained glass, it has been declared redundant and was vested in the Churches Conservation Trust in July 1987.

St Mary's Church, Totnes

Completed in 1450, this church was built on the site of a previous one which was dedicated in 1259, and partially restored in the nineteenth century by Sir George Gilbert Scott. It has a fifteenth-century stone screen, pulpit and font, with Victorian stained-glass windows and an organ originally built for the Great Exhibition in 1851.

MONASTIC HOUSES IN DEVON

The majority closed during the Dissolution of the Monasteries during the reign of Henry VIII, if not before.

Axminster Monastery (Saxon monastic community)
Axmouth Priory (Benedictine monks)
Barnstaple Priory (Cluniac monks)
Bodmiscombe Preceptory (Knights Templar)
Brightley Priory (Cistercian monks)
Buckfast Abbey (successively Savignac monks, Cistercian monks, then Benedictine monks)

Buckland Abbey (Cistercian monks)
Canonsleigh Abbey (Augustinian nuns)
Careswell Cell (Cluniac monks)
Chudleigh Abbey (Brigittine nuns)
Cornworthy Priory (Augustinian nuns)
Cowick Priory (Benedictine monks)
Dartmouth Priory (Augustinian friars)
Dunkeswell Abbey (Cistercian monks)
Exeter St Nicholas Priory (Benedictine monks)
Exeter Black Friary (Dominican friars)
Exeter Cathedral Priory (Benedictine monks)
Exeter Grey Friary (Franciscan friars)
Exeter Nunnery (Augustinian nuns)
Exeter St James Priory (Cluniac monks)
Frithelstock Priory (Augustinian Canons Regular)
Hartland Abbey (Augustinian Canons Regular)
Ipplepen Priory (Augustinian Canons Regular)
Kerswell Priory (Cluniac monks)
Leigh Cell, Leigh Grange, near Loddiswell (uncertain order)

Marsh Barton Priory (Augustinian Canons Regular)
Modbury Priory (Benedictine monks)
Newenham Abbey (Cistercian monks)
Otterton Priory (Benedictine monks)
Pilton Priory (Benedictine monks)
Plymouth Black Friary (Dominican Friars), site now occupied by
    Black Friars Distillery
Plymouth Grey Friary (Carmelite Friars)
Plymouth White Friary (Carmelite Friars)
Plympton Priory (Augustinian Canons Regular), now Priory
    Church of Saint Peter and Saint Paul, Plympton
Polsloe Priory, Exeter (Benedictine nuns)
Sidmouth Priory (Augustinian Canons Regular, Benedictine
    monks, later Brigittine monks)
St Austin's Priory, Ivybridge (Augustinian (Augustinian Recollect))
St Dunstan's Abbey, Plymouth
Tavistock Abbey (Benedictine monks)
Teignmouth Abbey (Benedictine nuns)
Torre Abbey (Premonstratensian Canons from Welbeck)
Totnes Priory (Benedictine monks)
Totnes Trinitarian Priory (Trinitarian monks)

SAXON & DANISH BATTLES

Although accounts of Devon history prior to medieval times
lack detail, battles or skirmishes are recorded as being fought
in various campaigns. The English and Saxons fought during
the latter's conquest of 'Dumnonia' as it was then known,
at Beaundun or Bindon, near Axmouth, in 614, the invaders
proving victorious, and killing an estimated 2,065 English. In 815
a Cornish raid at Galford near Lifton was beaten back. In 851
Danish invaders were repulsed by a force under the leadership of
Cedorl, an ealdorman of Devon, at Wucganbeorgh, thought to be
Weekaborough, near Torbay. In 876 Odda, another ealdorman,
and his army successfully fought off another Viking attack at
Countisbury, on Exmoor, although he and about 800 men were
killed. In a renewed Danish onslaught on Devon between about
990 and 1003, Tavistock, Kingsteignton and Exeter were all
sacked by the invaders.

THE ENGLISH CIVIL WAR

As in most of the rest of the country, the peers and gentry in Devon were mainly Royalist in their sympathies, while the others inclined towards the side of Parliament, with the general majority for Cromwell. The people of Plymouth had little reason to love King Charles I, largely as a result of its experiences at the time of the abortive expedition against Cadiz early in his reign when many of the defeated British soldiers died from starvation or disease, and the town's commerce suffered severely. Plymouth was besieged by Royalist forces who were eventually defeated. Queen Henrietta Maria stayed at the royal stronghold of Exeter and gave birth to a daughter there (see p. 8), but the king's forces in the West Country were defeated by 1646.

THE FIRST WORLD WAR

On 27 May 1918 the 2nd Battalion, the Devonshire Regiment, fought at the third Battle of the Aisne, France, against the German Spring Offensive, defending the Bois des Buttes, and lost 23 officers and 528 privates, all either dead or missing. Among them was the Commanding Officer, Colonel Rupert Anderson-Morshead. The battalion was awarded the French *Croix de Guerre*.

THE SECOND WORLD WAR

The first German bomb fell on Plymouth on 6 July 1940, leaving three people dead and injuring six. They were the first of 1,172 civilians killed and 3,276 injured during the next four years, giving the city the unhappy distinction of being the most bombed city in Britain per capita in terms of civilian casualties. Between 1940 and 1944 there were 602 air raid alerts and 59 actual bombing attacks, 3,754 houses were destroyed and a further 18,398 seriously damaged; 2 guildhalls, 6 hotels, 8 cinemas, 26 schools, 41 churches and 100 public houses were among buildings destroyed, while the old city centre was completely destroyed apart from St Andrew's Church, the Guildhall, the Regent Cinema (later demolished and replaced by Littlewoods store) and the *Western Morning News* offices.

In Exeter, there were 19 bombing raids between 1940 and 1942, in which 265 were killed and 788 injured. In 1942, as part of the Baedeker Blitz and specifically in response to the RAF bombing of Lübeck, 40 acres of the city, mainly the area adjacent to High Street and Sidwell Street, were destroyed, with the loss of several historic buildings, houses and shops.

On the south coast, Teignmouth suffered badly from 'tip and run' air raids. It was bombed 21 times between July 1940 and February 1944; in these raids 79 people were killed and 151 wounded, 228 houses were destroyed and over 2,000 damaged. Dartmouth, Torquay and Beesands also suffered casualties.

Newton Abbot was bombed several times between 1940 and 1942, with 22 killed and about 90 injured. The worst casualties were in August 1940 when three planes bombed the railway station, leaving 15 dead and 60 seriously injured.

DEVON IN WAR & PEACE

Her Majesty's Naval Base (HMNB) Devonport, is one of three remaining naval operating bases in the United Kingdom, the others being at Portsmouth and Clyde, and the largest naval base in Western Europe. It is also the only nuclear repair and refuelling facility for the Royal Babcock International Group, who took over from the previous owner, Devonport Management Ltd, in 2007.

FORMER RAF STATIONS IN DEVON

Babbacombe
Bolt Head
Chivenor
Dunkeswell
Exeter
Harrowbeer
Mount Batten (founded as Cattewater 1918, renamed 1928)
Roborough
Winkleigh

VICTORIA CROSS WINNERS

The Victoria Cross is the highest military decoration awarded for valour 'in the face of the enemy' to members of the armed forces of the United Kingdom, Commonwealth countries, and previous British Empire territories. The following recipients of the award are all buried in Devon (all apart from Hudson and Pennell were living in the county at the time of their death), although Fleming-Sandes was visiting friends in Hampshire at the time. Those marked * were also born in Devon.

Sir Redvers Buller* (1839–1908), General, 60th Rifles (King's Royal Rifle Corps), buried at Crediton

George Channer (1843–1905), General, 1st Gurkha Rifles, Bideford

Sir Henry Clifford (1826–83), Major-General, 1st Battalion Rifle Brigade, Ugbrooke House

Francis Farquharson (1837–75), Major, 42nd Regiment (Black Watch), Harberton

Arthur Fleming-Sandes (1894–1961), Major, 2nd Battalion East Surrey Regiment, Torquay (visiting at Romsey, Hampshire, at time of death)

Sir Gerald Graham (1831–99), Lieutenant-General, Corps of Royal Engineers, Bideford

Charles Grant (1861–1932), Brevet Colonel, 8th Gurkha Rifles, Sidmouth

Andrew Henry (1823–70), Captain, Royal Regiment of Artillery, Plymouth

George Hinckley (1819–1904), Quartermaster, Royal Navy, Plymouth

George Hollis (1833–79), Farrier, 8th Hussars (King's Royal Irish), Exeter

Charles Edward Hudson (1892–1959), Major-General, Comd. 11th Battalion, The Sherwood Foresters, Denbury

James Hutchinson (1895–1972), Corporal, 2/5th Battalion Lancashire Fusiliers, Torquay

James Johnson (1889–1943), Second Lieutenant, 2nd Battalion Northumberland Fusiliers, Plymouth

Edgar Myles (1894–1977), Captain, 8th Battalion Welch Regiment, Torquay

William Oxenham* (1823–75), Corporal, 32nd Regiment, Duke
  of Cornwall's Light Infantry, Exeter
Henry Pennell (1874–1907), Captain, 2nd Battalion Derbyshire
  Regiment, Dawlish
Peter Roberts (1917–79), Lieutenant, Royal Navy, Newton
  Ferrers
Thomas Sage* (1882–1945), Private, 8th Battalion Somerset
  Light Infantry, Tiverton
Gordon Steele* (1892–1981), Commander, Royal Navy,
  Winkleigh
Henry Sylvester (1831–1920), Surgeon Major, 23rd Regiment,
  Paignton
Alfred Toye (1897–1955), Brigadier, 2nd Battalion Middlesex
  Regiment, Tiverton

A memorial plaque was unveiled in Kingswear six months after
his death to Lieutenant-Colonel Herbert 'H' Jones (1940–82),
who was killed during the Falklands War and buried there. He
had spent part of his early life in the town.

THE STONE CROSS MEMORIAL

One of the most unusual individual war memorials is the Cave-
Penney Memorial or the Sherwell Cross, on Corndon Down, near
Poundsgate. It was erected in memory of Evelyn Anthony Cave-
Penney, a nineteen-year-old lieutenant in Queen Victoria's Own
Corps of Guides, who had lived with his family at Sherwell. He
fought with his infantry in Egypt and Palestine during the First
World War, and was shot dead by an enemy sniper on 8 June 1918.

GHOSTS, WITCHES & LEGENDS

The Berry Pomeroy ghost
Berry Pomeroy Castle near Totnes, built in the early twelfth
century, was home to the Pomeroy family from soon after the
Norman Conquest until 1549 when it passed to Sir Edward
Seymour, who built a mansion within the walls of the Norman

castle, though from the seventeenth century onwards it suffered during the Civil War and later fire, and little now remains. The dungeons are said to be haunted by the White Lady, who rises from St Margaret's Tower to the castle ramparts. She has been identified as the ghost of Lady Margaret Pomeroy who was imprisoned in the dungeons by her sister, Lady Eleanor. The latter was insanely jealous of her younger and prettier sister, and kept her captive because of a love rivalry, after Lord Pomeroy departed on a crusade and left Eleanor in charge. Margaret was imprisoned in the castle dungeons for nearly two decades, before Eleanor allowed her a slow and painful death through starvation. A blue light has been seen on a particular day every year in St Margaret's Tower, usually during the evening.

The Devil came down to Widecombe

On 21 October 1638, about 300 were packed inside St Pancras Church for Sunday service, when the sky turned pitch black and a fearful thunderstorm erupted. 'Extraordinary lightning came into the church so flaming that the whole church was presently filled with fire and smoke, the smell whereof was very loathsome, much like unto the scent of brimstone, some said at first they saw a great fiery ball come in through the window and pass through the church,' wrote one chronicler. A great ball of fire tore through a window, apparently blasting open the roof, tearing through the wall of the church tower and rebounding 'like a cannon ball', dislodging a pinnacle on the church tower which crashed through the roof, sending a large beam and building stones tumbling down. Many of the congregation were thrown to the ground, several were killed and about sixty injured. The ball of fire may have been a violent form of ball lightning, a rare and mysterious form sometimes seen in exceptionally intense thunderstorms. The Devil was apparently after Jan Reynolds, an unscrupulous local tin miner, who owed him money. On his way to Widecombe, a gentleman in a long black cape had called at the Tavistock Inn at Poundsgate, partly to ask for directions to the church and partly for a pint of ale. As he drank it, the other patrons heard it sizzle and saw steam as it went down his throat. As he passed the landlady a gold coin in payment, it turned into a leaf, went brittle and withered away. He then saddled his horse, rode to the church and tethered it outside, which was the moment at which the lightning struck.

The landlady of a nearby inn described how the Devil had passed through that day, and ordered ale that sizzled and steamed as he drank it. Tornados were often referred to as the Devil in those days, and it is thought that an exceptionally violent thunderstorm spawned both a tornado and ball lightning.

The wicked Lady Mary

Okehampton Castle was home to Lady Mary Howard, a seventeenth-century aristocrat who married four men (the first when she was only twelve years old) and allegedly killed each one of them, as well murdering maybe two of her children. Since her death, apparently from natural causes, she is condemned to travel nightly between Tavistock and Okehampton Castle, in a coach made of human bones from her victims, their skulls adorning the corners and the top. The coach is preceded by a huge black dog with one flaming eye in the middle of its forehead. Each night she must pluck a blade of grass from Okehampton Park, and only when all the grass is gone will she be set free again. Those who have seen the Lady have reported seeing images of her headless driving too.

Kitty Jay

The orphan Kitty Jay worked on a Dartmoor farm in the early nineteenth century and fell in love with the son of the house, who made her pregnant and then abandoned her. She then hanged herself in one of the barns. As she was a suicide, she could not be buried in consecrated ground, and was laid to rest at a crossroads near Manaton with a stake driven through her heart, so that her soul could not return to haunt the good Godfearing folk. In 1860 her bones were discovered while the road was being repaired, and reburied in the same place. Ever since then, freshly placed flowers appear on the site almost daily, placed there – it is said – by the Dartmoor piskies. People have reported seeing a dark figure wrapped in a cloak kneeling beside the grave, apparently the ghost of the farmer's son who is sentenced as an eternal punishment to stand vigil over the grave of Kitty and their unborn child.

The hairy hands

The B3212 near Two Bridges, southern Dartmoor, is renowned for its association with the 'hairy hands', which are said to have threatened drivers and even caused fatal accidents. In June 1921 Dr Helby, a medical officer who worked at Dartmoor Prison, was riding his motorcycle on his way to attend an inquest at Postbridge, with his two children in the sidecar. As he approached the bridge passing over the East Dart, he shouted at them to jump clear at once. They did so, just in time before he lost control of the vehicle and it crashed, leaving him with fatal injuries. A few weeks later a charabanc was on the same road when it suddenly swerved and mounted a slope on the right-hand side. Several passengers were thrown clear and one woman was seriously injured. The driver said afterwards that he was sure a pair of rough hairy hands had closed around him and driven him off the road.

Following an article in the *Daily Mail* in October 1921, authorities sent engineers to investigate the road, and the camber was made less deep. It did not put an end to similar incidents. In 1924 a young couple were sleeping in a caravan beside the road. During the night the woman awoke in a cold sweat, convinced she was in danger, and then saw a pair of hairy hands clawing at her partly open window. Keeping calm, she made the sign of the cross and they disappeared.

Ever since, motorists and cyclists have described similar incidents while on the same journey, while farmers with ponies and traps have said they have been forced into the verge. In 1961 a man from Plymouth died after overturning his car there, and in 1991 a Somerset doctor was injured in an accident which he described afterwards as if 'something evil' was in the car beside him, wrenching the steering wheel from his grasp.

Bideford witches
In 1682 a poor elderly woman, Temperance Lloyd, was arrested 'upon suspicion of having used some magical art, sorcery or witchcraft upon the body of Grace Thomas'. The meeting in front of the magistrates took place in Higher Gunstone, while Grace's illness consisted of a 'griping' in her 'belly, stomach and breast.' Grace Barnes was experiencing fits and Mary Trembles who was loitering outside Grace's house, was accused of being a witch along with another old woman, Susanna Edwards. Grace was carried to the town hall to give evidence, while Mary and Susanna

were sent to join Temperance at Exeter. At the trial on August 1682 they all pleaded not guilty, although they seemed to have freely confessed to their 'crimes' during cross-examination. They were found guilty and hanged on 25 August 1682 at Heavitree, among the last people to be executed in England for practising witchcraft.

The horsemen of Lustleigh Cleave

Hunters Tor, Lustleigh Cleave, on eastern Dartmoor, is reportedly haunted by phantom horsemen. The riders are dressed in medieval costume and their horses brightly decorated. Two other riders saw and followed them until the group disappeared behind a stone wall, after which there was no trace of them, and the only hoofprints discernible on the ground were those of the modern riders' animals. According to theory, the ghost horsemen were the Sheriff of Devon and twelve of his knights, ordered by King Henry III in 1240 to ride around the county boundaries to establish ownership.

Cranwell Pool

Also known as Crazywell, or Classiwell Pool, near Princetown, this water features strongly in local superstition. It is said that anybody who gazes into it on Midsummer's Eve will see the face of the next parishioner from nearby Walkhampton to die, and that those who walk within earshot of it at dusk will hear it call out the name of the next person to pass away. Somebody in a local pub was heard telling his friends the story, and two sceptical youths who overheard the conversation dismissed it as nonsense. They were challenged and told that they would not dare to visit the pool next Midsummer's Eve – but they accepted. As it was some distance by foot, they went by motorbike, and on the way back the vehicle sped off the road. Both were killed instantly.

The pool has been associated with bad luck ever since the fourteenth century when it was reputedly haunted by the Witch of Sheepstor, who always gave her clients bad advice. Piers Gaveston, the notorious favourite of King Edward II, was in Devon during a period of banishment from court, and she advised him to return to Warwick Castle, where 'his humbled head shall soon be high'. He did so, only to be captured by his enemies, beheaded, and his head placed high – on the battlements of the castle.

Sir Richard and Buckfastleigh Church

Richard Cabell, the local squire at Buckfastleigh, was believed to have murdered his wife and sold his soul to the devil. When he lay dying on 5 July 1677, it was said, hounds howled around his house waiting to take him to hell, and when he was buried, they returned to come and bay at his tomb. The villagers were so intent on laying his soul to rest that they laid a huge slab of stone on top of his tomb, and added a small house-like structure on top, to make sure he did not escape. Nevertheless, from time to time some have claimed to see a red glow shining through the bars. Every year on the anniversary of his death, tradition has it that he leads the phantom pack across the moors nearby, and can sometimes be seen riding in a coach led by a headless coachman and drawn by headless horses, with a pack of spectral hounds who came from the depths of the moor to escort his soul to hell chasing after them.

The church has attracted more than its fair share of bad luck. Being in a secluded location, in the early nineteenth century the graveyard was often raided by bodysnatchers, and in 1849 it was partly destroyed by arsonists. Restored in 1884, it fell victim to another arson attack in 1992 and was completely gutted.

The stranger at Down House Farm

At Down House Farm, half a mile outside Tavistock, the family was convinced that a ghost would appear one night, and so they always went to bed early in the hope that this would keep them safe from harm. On one such occasion, one of the boys was unwell and insisted he had to have a drink of water direct from the pump. Dreading she would meet the ghost, his mother went downstairs to fetch it for him. As she went she saw a shadow, heard footsteps behind her, and as she reached the pump she felt an icy hand on her shoulder. When she turned round, she saw a tall man standing there, and she asked him what he was doing. He asked her gently to watch him, as he promised that he was going to show her some hidden treasure. Lifting up the pump, he revealed a large quantity of money, which he urged her to take for herself and use for the good of the farm. He then told her that if anybody should attempt to deprive the family of the farm, they would pay dearly for it; and finally, that if she went and took the water to her boy, he would recover at once. Just then a cock crowed outside, the figure turned into a shadow, disappeared outside and turned into a small cloud.

The beast (or beasts) of Dartmoor

During the last thirty years or so, there has been much talk of sightings of big cats on Dartmoor, Devon's own equivalent of the Loch Ness monster. One theory is that the Dangerous Animals Act of 1976, which required owners of such animals to obtain a licence before keeping them in captivity, released them into the wild in order to spare themselves the bother. Another is that they have escaped from a travellers' camp. Yet another is that 'the Dartmoor beast(s)' owe more to a combination of rumour feeding rumour, and sheer imagination, than anything else. People claim to have seen large black animals (pumas or panthers), large sandy-brown animals (lions), huge paw prints and skulls, and dead sheep and ponies with injuries that could only have been caused by such predators. For every person who believes there are fierce wild creatures running around on the moor, there is at least one other who points to the likelihood of their merely being large dogs seen from a distance, with foxes having been responsible for the killings. The present author recalls his mother sometimes taking a large golden Labrador retriever out while walking on the southern edges of the moor, and at least once this coincided with a story in the news about somebody having definitely seen the 'Dartmoor lion'. There is a British county league table of big cat sightings in the wild, and Devon is ranked fourth.

HAUNTED PUBS

The Bishop Lacey Inn, Chudleigh
A former landlord at the fourteenth-century inn, the oldest in Chudleigh, was closing up one night as a cloaked figure came through the door and went upstairs, disregarding the signs saying 'Private'. He called out but the visitor took no notice. His wife came downstairs to ask him who he was talking to, and when he explained, she told him that nobody was there. However, guests subsequently heard unexplained footsteps around the premises. A couple of years later, a married couple and their son came to the inn where they intended to stay for three days, but after hearing and sensing a strange presence during the night, checked out and left hurriedly next morning. The character is supposed to be either a monk or Edmund Lacey, Bishop of Exeter, himself.

Old Smugglers' Inn, Coombe Cellars, near Teignmouth
A live-in barmaid woke night after night, terrified that although she had locked her bedroom, she was not alone. The landlord told her she was imaging things, until he found some old prints of the pub at a local auction. One of them clearly showed a woman being murdered by an intruder – in what was identifiably the same bedroom as the one occupied by his barmaid.

The Pig and Whistle, Littlehempston, near Totnes
A special chair was reserved by the fireside in the bar for 'Freddie', a hunchbacked smiling monk, who would appear through a window where there used to be a door. Although very few people would admit to having seen him, many of those who knew the story heard and saw the window open and assume that he was arriving. One, more fortunate (if that is the right word) than most, a clairvoyant from Plymouth who came in for a drink one evening with his wife, told the landlady afterwards that he had seen the figure of a monk following her around the bar.

Church House Inn, Torbryan, near Newton Abbot
One night the landlord was locking up, when his dog's hackles rose and the cat arched her back as they stared at something in the corner of the bar. The cat shot upstairs, though she had never

done so before, and for several nights afterwards, the dog would stand on the landing at exactly the same time each evening, and bark. Another landlord told of staying awake in his bedroom with his wife on New Year's Eve to welcome in the New Year, when they heard the door open at the bottom of the stairs, followed by footsteps. They called out, assuming their son had just returned early from a rather disappointing party, but there was no answer. Their son did call out as he arrived back – five hours later.

LEGENDARY CREATURES

Dartmoor pixies, or piskies, are small mythological creatures usually portrayed with pointed ears. They are said to love riding on Dartmoor ponies, enjoy music and dancing, and reputedly have a mischievous sense of humour in that they sometimes mislead unwary travellers across the moor into bogs. The only defence against being 'pixie-led' is for people to turn their coats inside out first. During the Civil War, it is said, a member of the staunchly Royalist Elford family at Tavistock took refuge from Cromwell's troops on Dartmoor in a pixie house, a natural cavern on Sheepstor.

Pixie Day takes place at Ottery St Mary every year on the Saturday nearest to Midsummer's Day, commemorating the banishment of the pixies from the town where they caused trouble to a local cave on the banks of the Otter known as 'Pixies' Parlour'. It begins with a large fête, followed by local children dressed in pixie costumes going to drag the bellringers from the church to the town square for a re-enactment of the banishment, and finally a fireworks display.

Dartmoor and Exmoor are home to the 'wisht hounds', or black dogs with staring eyes, who hunt down unbaptised souls.

The Dewerstone, near Shaugh Bridge, is traditionally the site where footprints in the snow, one human, another of cloven hoofs, showed where Dewer (the devil) led a traveller over a cliff edge in a blizzard.

The popular Dartmoor song, 'Widecombe Fair', which purports to be about taking people to market on Tom Pearse's grey mare, is sometimes said to be a dark tale about taking souls to the devil.

LOCAL CUSTOMS

Widecombe Fair

Widecombe Fair, as immortalised in the song with its refrain of 'Old Uncle Tom Cobley an' all', takes place annually on the second Tuesday in September. The earliest reference that can be traced to it is a reference in a Plymouth newspaper of about 1850 calling it a cattle fair. Later it became an opportunity to show and sell other livestock, and in about 1920 sports for local schoolchildren were also introduced. In 1933 stalls for rural arts and crafts were added. It was suspended during the Second World War but revived in 1945, including for the first time a gymkhana and a tug-of-war contest. Apart from cancellation during 2001 after an outbreak of foot and mouth disease, it has continued ever since. During the early years it was held in various locations around the village, and nowadays it is staged in a large field south of the village, with adjacent fields used for parking. It also includes a dog show and vintage farm machinery.

Guy Fawkes' Day

On 5 November, two Devon towns have their own unique and very different customs. One is at Shebbear, where people turn the devil's stone in order to avert bad luck for another year. The stone, about 6ft long and weighing at least a ton, is said to have been dropped by the devil when he was expelled from heaven. A more prosaic explanation is that it was quarried as a foundation stone for Hanscott church nearby and was moved to Shebbear by the devil or some other supernatural powers, then taken away at intervals but always mysteriously returned to Shebbear. In 1940 most able-bodied men were away on war service and the custom fell into abeyance, but next year the news of the war became so bad that, ever since then, the locals have not dared to let it slip by again.

The other is at Ottery St Mary, where 5 November means Tar Barrels, which are soaked in tar for several weeks before the event. During the evening they are lit outside the town's four pubs, and when the flames start to pour out, people (who have to have been born in the town or lived there most of their lives) carry them over their shoulders. Those who are mouthing the words 'risk assessment' or 'Health and Safety' may rest assured that the event is carefully stewarded to ensure maximum safety, and throughout the evening roads in and out of the town are closed to traffic.

Worm Charming

The annual Worm Charming Festival is held every May Day Bank Holiday in a field in Blackawton, the exact site not being revealed in advance just in case anybody should try to introduce an unduly large number of worms into the soil beforehand. Contestants tap or dance on the ground, and water, beer, cider, gravy or sugar are applied to try to bring them up to the surface. They are not allowed to dig, but can otherwise use any means to catch them as long as they do them no physical harm. They have to sample the liquids first in order to prove that they contain no noxious substances or poison. Fancy dress is encouraged and prizes are awarded for the best costume, while other attractions include or have included a beer festival, ram roasts, Morris and maypole dancing, various games and car boot sales.

Tavistock Goosey Fair

This tradition dating back to the early twelfth century has been held every second Wednesday in October since 1823. It attracts market traders and showmen from throughout the country, with over 200 stalls and sideshows set up in the town centre. Farmers

used to drive their geese through the streets to the market, though this practice has stopped partly for ethical reasons, and partly because of the incidence of fowlpest in the second half of the twentieth century. A song 'Tavistock Goozey Vair' was published in 1912 by C. John Trythall, although nobody is certain whether he wrote it or was simply the first to publish an old song which had been handed down from previous generations.

The Devon County Show

The Devon County Show is an agricultural show held annually over three days in May. It began in 1872, when the Devon County Agricultural Association was formed to promote such an event, and was held at different sites around the county until 1956, when it moved to a regular site at Whipton. It moved to its present site at the Westpoint Arena and Showground, Clyst St Mary, in 1990. In 1981 it was almost called off for the first time in its history because of bad weather. A long spell of heavy rain had turned the site into a quagmire, and on the eve of its opening on 20 May, officials met to make a decision. They went ahead with the show, employing a convoy of lorries working round the clock to deliver tons of gravel to spread on the worst-affected areas. The jumping events which were to have been held in the main ring were cancelled, and the closure of some fields which would have been used for parking resulted in long traffic queues. A bill of over £25,000 for sand and gravel, and poor attendances of 61,252 as opposed to 91,604 the previous year, resulted in a substantial loss for the organisers.

Sidmouth Folk Week

Sidmouth Folk Week, previously Sidmouth International Festival, is held annually in the first week of August and includes concerts, ceilidhs, workshops, dance displays and children's activities. It was founded as a folk dance festival in 1955 by the English Folk Dance and Song Society (EFDSS), and expanded to cover ceilidh dancing, music, song and related folk crafts. After widening its scope to include performers from abroad, it was renamed the Sidmouth International Folklore Festival. In 1986, the management was taken over by a new company which renamed it Sidmouth International Festival and ran it for 18 years, attracting about 65,000 visitors annually. A change of management in 2004 saw it take its present name.

Dartmoor Folk Festival

This was founded in 1978 by local musician Bob Cann who saw it as a means of helping to revive and preserve the traditions of Dartmoor, and the traditional music, dance, song and crafts of the area. The first three festivals were held in the grounds of Wood Country House near South Tawton, before it moved to its present location in South Zeal in 1981.

Several other annual events are held in the county, among them Chagstock (the Chagford UK Music Festival), Bideford Folk Festival and the Teignmouth Folk and Jazz Festivals.

Until the early eighteenth century, when a tenant cottager in High Bickington died, the lord of the manor would claim the best beast for 'herriot', and any widow who retained the tenancy must remain chaste, in other words not remarry, or else the tenancy would be forfeited. If this occurred, she could regain it by attending the Court Baron, bestriding a ram back to front, and holding its tail while reciting her offence as she prayed to be readmitted to her land.

DEVON FLAGS & COATS OF ARMS

The Devon flag was created in 2002 as a result of a vote on the BBC Devon website, with the winning design by student Ryan Sealey, who allegedly produced it on his home computer in about ten minutes, taking 49 per cent of the votes. Its predominantly green colour represents that of the rolling hills, the black the high windswept moorland, and the white the salt spray of both coastlines and the China Clay industry. In October 2006 Devon County Council raised the flag outside County Hall for the first time.

In April 2004 Rodney Lock, of Ottery St Mary, had been threatened with legal action for flying a Devon flag in his back garden, and faced a £60 charge to get planning permission from East Devon District Council. A spokesman said they had received a complaint and had no choice but to investigate the matter. As a result, the Minister for Housing ruled that authorities could officially 'turn a blind eye' to the practice of flying county flags from poles.

WHEN THE DEVON FLAG CAN OFFICIALLY BE FLOWN

The Devon Flag Group (DFG), a non-profit-making organisation set up in 2003 to promote the use of the flag, has recommended the following as appropriate dates, based on local events and the feast days of saints with particular county relevance.

4 January – St Rumon of Tavistock and Romansleigh
7 January – St Brannock of Braunton
5 March – St Piran, patron saint of tin miners
7 April – St Brannock, celebrated on this day in Exeter
May – May Day Bank Holiday; anniversary of first time Devon
    Flag was flown at World Gig Championship, Isles of Scilly,
    2003; Devon County Show
3 June – St Kevin, educated by St Petroc
4 June – St Petroc, for whom the flag is dedicated
5 June – St Boniface of Crediton
6 June – St Gudwal, hermit of Devon
17 June – St Nectan, patron of Hartland
21/2 June – Midsummer's Day
8 July – St Urith
13 July – St Juthware
30 July – Anniversary of defeat of Spanish Armada
August – St Sidwell, virgin of Exeter
10 August – St Geraint of Dumnonia
30 August – St Rumon
28 September – Anniversary of Sir Francis Drake's
    circumnavigation of the world
2 November – St Cumgar
5 November – St Kea
7 November – St Congar
8 December – St Budoc (Budeaux) of Plymouth
12 December – St Corentin
21/2 December – Midwinter
31 December–6 January – New Year's Eve to Twelfth Night

PLYMOUTH'S COAT OF ARMS

Plymouth's coat of arms, designed by Arthur Cockrane, Clarenceux King of Arms, and authorised in 1931, consists of a silver spade-shaped shield with a green St Andrew's Cross (the dedication of the Mother Church of Plymouth) and four black towers representing the towers of the original Plymouth Castle. The crest is a blue naval crown, and a red anchor held aloft by a golden lion's paw, taken from the old Devonport arms and representing the naval connection. The two lion supporters, with red medallions charged with a silver boar's head, are taken from the arms of the Mount Edgcumbe family, who held the Manor of East Stonehouse. The motto, 'Turris fortissima est nomen Jehova', translates as 'The name of Jehovah is the strongest tower', from the Proverbs of Solomon.

EXETER'S COAT OF ARMS

Confirmed by William Hervey, Clarenceux King of Arms during a visit to Devon in 1564, Exeter's arms depict the long-vanished Rougemont Castle, with the distinctive form of the castle described in the blazon as 'triangular and triple towered'. The red and black colouring of the field has no apparent significance. The crest wreath is black and gold, the colours of the Duchy of Cornwall, the crest itself being a red crowned lion holding a golden orb, for Richard, Earl of Cornwall, Holy Roman Emperor. The same lion appears in the arms of Devon County Council and some of the towns and districts of Devon. The supporters are winged horses or pegasuses, the wings are charged with blue waves, representing the River Exe. The motto 'Semper Fidelis' (Ever Faithful) was suggested by Elizabeth I in a letter addressed to the citizens of Exeter in 1588 in recognition of a gift of money towards the fleet that defeated the Spanish Armada.

TORBAY'S COAT OF ARMS

Torbay's arms, granted on 12 May 1968, are a simple map of Torbay, the gold enarched chief representing the sandy beaches, and the blue field the sea. The ship represents the maritime interests of the borough, while the St George's flag and streamers recall the area's historic links with the Royal Navy. From the masthead hangs a cross composed of the stocks of four anchors, suggesting the fusion of four maritime councils in one. Each arm of the cross resembles a letter T for Torbay. On the chief is a mural crown, symbol of local government, and showing the borough situated on Tor Bay. The crown is red, the colour of Devon earth, and has four crenellations for the four old councils. The blue and gold livery colours refer to the sea and sands. Blue also featured in the arms or devices of Torquay, Paignton and Brixham, and these are also the livery colours of the arms of Nassau, commemorating the landing of William of Orange at Brixham. Dolphins, featured in the crests of Paignton and Torquay, are often found in the arms of seaside towns. The crosier is from the arms of Torre Abbey, and the horseshoe, from the Ferrers family arms, represents Churston Ferrers. The supporters, sealions, are derived from the sinister supporter of the arms of Devon County Council. The leonine part of the supporters is coloured red, like the lion in the arms of the County Council. Each supporter is differenced by a cable around the neck from which hangs a Tau cross. This suggests the initial T of the Borough's name, and also sounds like the word 'Tor', which names the bay. The motto, 'Salubritas Et Felicitas', means Health and Happiness.

MID-DEVON'S COAT OF ARMS

The Mid-Devon shield has a background of white and blue waves indicating the rivers of the district, and over them lies a chief across the top and a pale down the middle, both coloured red for the Devon earth. At the top is a stylised castle in gold, suggested by that in the Tiverton borough seal, between two gold wheatsheaves indicating agriculture, denoting the former Borough and Rural District of Tiverton. On the pale is a crosier alluding to St Boniface of Crediton. He is said to have cut down a huge oak tree sacred to Thor, and the oak is associated with him in sacred art. His episcopal staff is shown entwined with a branch of oak also in gold, this also being a reference to the rural area around Crediton. The shield thus represents all four areas of the former authorities. The crest is a span of the district's history from medieval to modern industrial times. The blue lion is that of the Radvers Earls of Devon, one of whom, Richard, built Tiverton Castle in the early twelfth century. He holds the woolpack from the Borough Seal, indicating the importance of the woollen industry in this area in earlier times. The woolpack is charged with a steel cogwheel for industry and engineering. The motto 'Fide et Industria' translates as 'By Faith and Diligence', or 'By Faith and Industry'.

DARTMOUTH'S COAT OF ARMS

Dartmouth's coat of arms bear the symbolic representation of a king, probably Edward III, who granted the town a charter in 1341. On either side is a seated lion. The ship, king and lions are all tinctured gold, as recognition of the town's provision of ships for the naval campaigns in the Hundred Years' War, as well as the assembly of a fleet for Richard I's invasion of the Holy Land. The borough was originally constituted under a charter of King Henry II as 'the Borough of Clifton Dartmouth and Hardness'. The seal was recorded by the borough at the heralds' visitation of Devon in 1620, and the design was confirmed as the borough arms by a King of Arms Certificate in January 1951.

10

DEVON EXPLORERS & ECCENTRICS

EXPLORERS

Sir Francis Drake (*c*. 1540–96), born at Crowndale, near Tavistock, is arguably Devon's (if not Britain's) most famous sea dog. His achievements included completing the first circumnavigation of the world by an Englishman, from which he returned in 1580, and as one of the captains instrumental in defeating the Spanish Armada in 1588. Perhaps appropriately, he died of disease off the coast of Panama during an expedition to the Caribbean. His statues are to be seen on Plymouth Hoe and at Tavistock. His cousin Sir John Hawkins (1532–95) took part in several of the same overseas ventures, and died of a similar illness on the same expedition. Drake took a snare drum with him, emblazoned with his coat of arms, when he sailed round the world. It was with him as he lay on his deathbed off the coast of Panama in 1596, and he ordered that it should be returned to his home at Buckland Abbey (where it remains to this day), so that it could be beaten to recall him from heaven when he should be needed to come to the nation's rescue whenever England was in danger. Since then, people have claimed to hear it beating when the *Mayflower* sailed from England in 1620, when Napoleon was brought into Plymouth Sound as a prisoner, and on the outbreak of the First World War. When the German navy surrendered in 1918, a drum roll was heard on board the battleship HMS *Royal Oak* as she escorted German ships from the high seas fleet to their internment in Scapa Flow. The ship was thoroughly searched but no drum was found, and everyone assumed that it must have been Drake's Drum. It was also heard in 1940 at the time of the evacuation of Dunkirk.

Sir Humphrey Gilbert (*c.* 1539–83), born at Greenway, near Galmpton, was a pioneer of colonisation in England and North America. The majority of his maritime expeditions were failures, and he was lost at sea when his ship sank in a storm near the Azores.

Sir Richard Grenville (1542–91), born probably at Buckland Abbey, was charged with maintaining a fleet at the Azores to waylay Spanish treasure fleets. At Flores he was taken by surprise by a large fleet from Spain. His crew had just been depleted by sickness and he had an opportunity of escape, but chose to try to fight his way out of the impasse. He died from his wounds, with his ship sinking soon afterwards.

John Davis (*c.* 1550–1605), born at Sandridge, near Dartmouth, navigator and explorer in mainly polar regions, is sometimes credited with discovering the Falkland Islands in about 1592. He was killed by Japanese pirates off the Malay peninsula.

William John Wills (1834–61), born at Totnes, was surveyor and later promoted to second-in-command on an expedition across Australia led by Robert O'Hara Burke. Setting out from

Melbourne in August 1860, they succeeded in crossing largely uncharted territory to the north coast, thus completing the first overland crossing, but through a combination of poor leadership, bad planning and misfortune, both men perished from exposure and malnutrition ten months later on the return journey. One man from the expedition, John King, lived to tell the tale and was found by a rescue party just in time.

Sir Robert Falcon Scott (1868–1912), born at Outland House, Plymouth, led the first British Antarctic expedition on HMS *Discovery* between 1901 and 1904, during which time he made the first balloon flight on the sub-continent. In 1911 he led a team which aimed to be the first to reach the South Pole, but were beaten to it by an expedition led by the Norwegian Roald Amundsen in January 1912, by about a fortnight. Scott and his surviving team perished at the end of March, and their bodies were found by a rescue party eight months later.

Percy Harrison Fawcett (1867–c. 1925), born at Torquay and thought to be the original inspiration behind movie character Indiana Jones, as played by actor Harrison Ford, was both explorer and eccentric. A couple of expeditions undertaken in Bolivia and Brazil for surveying for minerals on behalf of both countries' respective governments were interrupted by service during the First World War. Several years later he returned to Brazil to search for 'Z', in pursuit of 'hidden cities' and more minerals, but no trace of him, his expedition or the missing cities has been found to this day.

Frank (Francis) Bickerton (1889–1954), born in Oxfordshire, moved to Plymouth during childhood and lived there until 1920. He took part in an Australasian Antarctic Expedition 1911–14 as an engineer, was responsible for the pioneering use of an aeroplane and wireless telegraphy in the Antarctic, and led a sledging expedition which discovered the first meteorite found there. He fought on the Western Front during the First World War, and later served with the Royal Flying Corps and the Royal Air Force.

ECCENTRICS

Joanna Southcott (*c.* 1750–1814) was born in Taleford near Ottery St Mary. For some years she worked as a domestic servant. Having been brought up as a Methodist, when she was about forty she claimed to have heard a voice foretelling a solution to the world's problems with the imminent arrival of the second coming of Jesus Christ. She was almost illiterate, and the messages she received were generally dictated to and copied by the friends and supporters she called her secretaries. She was ignored by the established church, representatives of which were convinced she was a fraud. Their suspicions were doubtless justified by her remarkable ability to make a healthy sum by selling 'Certificates for the Millennium', and 'Sealings for the Faithful', passports to heaven, at prices between 12*s* and 1 guinea. The writer Sabine Baring-Gould called her 'a shameless impostor', and regarding the books, manuscripts and letters she wrote (or dictated) and published, his verdict was that 'it is not possible to conceive that any persons could have been deluded by such rambling nonsense.' Yet there were enough gullible souls around, and she attracted a following of several thousand. In 1792 she had published a prophecy stating that one day she would give birth, prior to which she would be dead for four days, then revive, and be delivered.

In 1814, after she had moved to London, she proclaimed that the Spirit had told her that 'in the sixty-fifth year of thy age, thou shalt have a Son, by the power of the Most High'. In preparation for her virgin birth she was examined by over twenty doctors, some declaring she was pregnant while others dismissing the idea as absurd. The birth was due on 19 October 1814, but the day came and went, and it was announced that she had gone into a trance. She died at her home on 26 or 27 December, and her disciples retained her body for four days, wrapped it in flannel and kept it warm with hot water bottles. They expected her to come to life, but after four days the corpse stubbornly not only refused to breathe, but also showed signs of discoloration. Only after signs of visible decay were no longer in doubt did they agree to the burial of her body. It was rumoured, though not confirmed, that a post-mortem had been conducted and revealed that she was suffering from dropsy.

The architect **John Foulston** (1772–1841), creator of some of the most striking Plymouth and Devonport buildings of the early nineteenth century (see p. 23), who lived at Mutley, Plymouth, not only loved ancient classical civilisation but did his best to live up to it as well. He used to drive around the streets of the town in a gig disguised as a Roman war chariot.

The **Revd William Buckland** (1784–1856), born at Axminster and educated at Blundell's School, Tiverton, was a noted geologist and palaeontologist. He was the first ever Professor of Geology at Oxford University, and was later Dean of Westminster. He was also famous for keeping a variety of animals, some dangerous, inside his house. Some of them probably met an early death before going into the oven, as he was apparently determined to try to eat every animal ever discovered at least once. He generously found praiseworthy qualities in all of them except the mole, which he found disgusting. It was said that his breath sometimes smelt of crocodile, hedgehog and roast joint of bear and puppy (please do not trust this man with your pets). John Ruskin once regretted, probably with tongue-in-cheek, having missed the chance to eat mice on buttered toast. He was the world's leading authority on coprolites, or fossilised faeces, but as he had coined the word himself, there was not much competition for the honour. A dining table made entirely out of said matter was one of his prized (by him if nobody else) possessions. He claimed to have eaten the heart of King Louis XIV of France, which had come from his grave during the French Revolution and into the possession of his friend the Archbishop of York. His sole comment was that it would have been improved with gravy made from the blood of a marmoset monkey.

By the time he reached his sixties he began to behave oddly, though some felt he had been doing so for years anyway, beating himself around the head and scratching himself until he bled. He ended his days in a lunatic asylum in Clapham, though posterity does not relate whether he was still allowed to do his own cooking or order his choice of meat.

The mathematician and scientist **Oliver Heaviside** (1850–1925) was born in London, but spent most of his adult life in Devon.

He had worked briefly as a telegraph operator at home and abroad before deciding to devote the rest of his life to research and writing technical papers. His books were well respected but well nigh unintelligible, and when it was pointed out to him that they could do with editing as they were so hard to read, he pointed out that they were even harder to write. His brother Charles was a partner in a music business in Torquay, and when another store in Paignton was opened in 1889, he invited Oliver and their parents to leave London and come to live above the shop. Oliver himself took over the second floor as a laboratory for his daily experiments, and took up cycling on a machine which used metal spoons for brakes.

After his parents died in 1897 he moved to Newton Abbot. By now strange stories about his odd behaviour began to circulate. Always a very private individual, and convinced that neighbours were prying into his affairs, he described them in a letter to a friend as 'the rudest lot of impertinent, prying people that I have ever had the misfortune to live near. They talk the language of the sewer and seem to glory in it.' He lived for some time on a diet of tinned milk and biscuits, and claimed that he suffered from 'hot and cold' disease, turning the gas fire up full in winter to keep warm enough. Visitors to the house, who became more infrequent as time went on, found it unbearably hot. As his health declined, he was less able to look after himself properly.

In 1908 he moved back to Torquay, in a house owned by his brother's sister-in-law, Mary Way. Mindful of his strange ways, she agreed to take him as a paying guest, but some years later she had had enough and moved out, leaving him on his own. Visitors would find his door and trees covered with documents, many of them summonses for non-payment of rates and outstanding accounts from what he called 'the Gas Barbarians'. His scientific achievements did not go unrecognised, and in 1922 he became the first recipient of the newly established Faraday Medal. When he was advised that a delegation of four would be visiting him at home to present him with the award, he wrote back to insist that they should all come separately on different days. In the end they agreed to send just one.

Three years later he fell off a ladder, was rushed to hospital and died from complications to his injuries. He was buried in the family grave at Paignton Cemetery. Later several unpublished scientific papers in his own hand were discovered under the floorboards at his house. He had put them there to act as insulation.

The Dartmoor author and campaigner **Beatrice Chase**, whose real name was Olive Katherine Parr (1874–1955), was born in Middlesex, but moved to Widecombe-on-the-Moor as a young woman. She wrote several titles, including *The Heart of the Moor* (1914), *Through a Dartmoor Window* (1915), and *Pages of Peace from Dartmoor* (1920), which were very popular for a brief period. Her fiancé was killed in the First World War, and she became increasingly religious. She maintained a personal chapel at Venton House, her home, where she initiated her Knights of the White Crusade, encouraging all servicemen to be 'pure and noble'. When she took up photography, she signed a contract with postcard publisher Raphael Tuck to produce local views for his cards. Later she became embittered and reclusive, suffered from persecution mania, accused booksellers (and Tuck) of profiteering, and took to selling books and postcards directly to visitors to her home, but as her fortunes dwindled and her style of writing fell out of favour, she was reduced to selling signed books to friends at a large discount. She was eventually diagnosed with cancer and taken to Newton Abbot Infirmary, and according to locals she was removed in a straitjacket, after the loaded revolver she kept by her bedside was removed.

The artist **Robert Lenkiewicz** (1941–2002), who spent most of his working life in a studio in the Barbican, Plymouth, was legendary for his unorthodox methods. He once painted a large mural on the waterfront in which he got his own back on some council officials who had thwarted or irritated him in various ways, by portraying them prominently – in the nude. In 1981 he prematurely announced his own death in *The Times* because he was preparing for a project of paintings on the theme of death, and although he could not know how it felt to be dead, he wanted to see how it felt if others thought he had died.

One of his friends and models was Albert Fisher, whom he called 'The Bishop'. The artist called him 'an extraordinary man with large hands and a great red beard, who slept beneath a tree in Stoke Damerel graveyard and believed he had had mystical experiences. He came rushing in one day and said that the sun had been shining through the tree, that every single leaf had turned into a man with a top hat, that each man with a top hat had a pint of beer in his hand and that each and every one of them had wished him 'Good morning!' In the posh Oxford accent he had cultivated, he said, 'I had a *vision* there. Not a dream, not a nightmare but a *vision* there!' The present author, who was an assistant in Plymouth Central Reference Library during the early 1970s, recalls 'The Bishop' as a very ruddy-faced, regular visitor to read the papers and occasionally cross verbal swords with the then Head of Reference Services, who objected to the pungent aroma of alcohol which emanated from his direction and his unmistakable loud voice. There was no love lost between both men. Another friend was 'Diogenes', whose real name was Edward McKenzie. Lenkiewicz gave him his new name after a Greek philosopher who lived in a barrel, after finding him living in a concrete pipe at Chelson Meadow rubbish tip while working on a project about down-and-outs. Shortly before his death in 1984, aged seventy-two, he was promised by the artist that he would preserve his body as a 'human paperweight' and not hand him over to the authorities for burial. He was as good as his word. Not only did he have Diogenes embalmed, but he stubbornly refused to tell officials from Plymouth City Council where the body was, despite the environmental health department's determination to have him properly buried. He invited them to his studio where they found a coffin which they expected to contain Diogenes' body – until Lenkiewicz himself jumped out. A spokesman said the affair had degenerated into music-hall farce, yet they still meant to find the body. One year later the council admitted defeat.

Ten days after Lenkiewicz died in August 2002, in a secret drawer in his studio was the supposedly missing enbalmed corpse. Also in the artist's 'death room' were the skeleton of Ursula Kemp, a sixteenth-century midwife who was hanged for witchcraft and nailed into her coffin, kept in a long wooden box on top of the piano, and a parchment lampshade (don't ask any further) which he claimed had been brought out of Auschwitz in 1940, on the desk. On 11 October Nigel Meadows, the Plymouth Coroner, revealed that Lenkiewicz had been as good as his word. Since its discovery, the body had been kept in a hospital mortuary awaiting a decision on what should happen to it. Mr Meadows conceded that Diogenes was 'nicely preserved', and said it was up to the executor of the Lenkiewicz estate to have the body cremated or transferred to the Lenkiewicz Foundation, the charity responsible for the artist's paintings and books, and then up to the foundation to decide what to do with the body. 'Provided they comply with health and safety regulations and don't outrage public decency,' he said, 'it is possible that they could retain the body on some sort of public display.'

In September 2010, the national press reported that an elderly, bearded gentleman, calling himself **Moses-Peter**, was doing his bit to make the world a better place. Every day, for some years, he had donned beads and a headband, and sat on a chair on the A3022 between Torquay and Paignton, waving and smiling at drivers and bus passengers. During the Christmas season he also wore a Santa hat and tinsel on his stick. Motorists set up a site on Facebook for him, called 'Strange old man who sits on a bench on the road between Torquay and Paignton', which attracted thousands of supporters and messages from admirers who said he had made their day. When it was revealed that he did not have a computer and therefore could not access the internet, a comment was posted suggesting that he ought to be given a BlackBerry for Christmas. Very publicity-shy, when asked why he was doing this, he merely answered, 'I am spreading a message of joy, love and happiness.'

JOLLY JAPES

On 1 April 1949 a Plymouth solicitor received a telegram, purporting to come from a well-known local agricultural firm. It informed him that ten tons of farmyard manure were going to be delivered at his house that morning and would he kindly make arrangements to store it. He was horrified – until his wife reminded him what the date was.

In 1997, exactly 48 years later, the *Western Evening Herald* announced that M. Poisson d'Avril, of La Pofloir, was planning to set up a French vineyard in the St Budeaux area of Plymouth. He had discovered that he could beat the quota system on vine production if he chose a district outside France which sounded suitably French. The gentleman's name, and a swift rearrangement of the letters in 'La Pofloir', revealed all, and several readers saw through it at once.

In the 1960s, a pathway in South Brent which led to a path alongside the River Avon used to have a NO THROUGH ROAD sign near the entrance. In due course somebody either rearranged the letters or did a skilful repainting job, with the result that it then read NO ROUGHTOAD. At around the same time, a short-lived local community journal, *Bravo Brent!*, carried a few verses from a local contributor, about 'Roughtoad', in which the eponymous beast was portrayed as a demon who would come and get naughty children if they did not do as they were told.

On a similar theme, in March 2011, a skilled signwriter with a sense of humour overpainted a triangular GIVE WAY sign with the words WAKE UP, and attached beneath it a rectangular sign saying WORLD CRISIS AHEAD. The 10ft sign was placed on the road from a bridge at Staverton, near Totnes, just before the junction with the A384 near Huxhams Cross. A spokesman for Devon County Council said they were looking into what could be described as a vandal attack, and that it would be removed as soon as possible. 'We weren't aware of it until you told us about it,' he told a press reporter who asked for a statement, 'but it sounds like it shouldn't be there.'

In February 2011 Dr Geri Parlby, a lecturer at Exeter University, suggested that recent claims that 8,000-year-old Cornish cave paintings showed prehistoric women eating pasties were no more than 'a fine example of the Cornish practical joke'.

11

SPORTING DEVON

SPORTING PERSONALITIES

Sir Francis Chichester (1901–72), born at Barnstaple, was the first person to sail solo around the world, from east to west and around

the great capes. He circumnavigated the world in *Gipsy Moth IV* between August 1966 and May 1967, departing from and returning to Plymouth. His success inspired another would-be round-the-world yachtsman, Donald Crowhurst (1932–69), who sailed from Teignmouth in October 1968 in *Teignmouth Electron* trimaran, while competing in the *Sunday Times* Golden Globe Race, but his attempts were believed to have ended in insanity and suicide about eight months later, although his body was never found.

Cliff Bastin (1912–91), footballer with Exeter FC and later Arsenal, retired in 1947 and returned to his home city of Exeter, where he and his wife ran a café and then a pub.

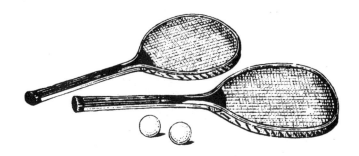

Angela Mortimer (1932–), born at Plymouth, former No. 1 British female tennis player, winner of three Grand Slam singles titles, at 1955 French championships, 1958 Australian championships, and at Wimbledon in 1961.

Ian Roberts (1948–) represented Devon in 26 championship cricket matches 1974–80.

Trevor Francis (1954–), born at Plymouth, joined Birmingham City FC and later Nottingham Forest, becoming England's first £1,000,000 footballer.

Sue Barker (1956–), born at Paignton, whose professional career included her reaching the semi-finals at Wimbledon. After retiring from professional tennis she became a successful broadcaster and commentator.

Sharron Davies (1962–), born at Plymouth, Olympic and Commonwealth games swimmer turned commentator.

Professional Football Teams
Plymouth Argyle FC (founded 1886, as Argyle FC)
Torquay United FC (1899)
Exeter City FC (1904)

Professional Rugby Football Teams
Plymouth Albion (founded 1875)
Exeter Chiefs (1871)

Rugby League Teams
Plymouth Titans (founded 2003)
Exeter Centurions (2007)
Devon Sharks, Torquay (2006)
East Devon Eagles, Exmouth (2006)

Basketball
Plymouth Raiders (founded 1978)
Plymouth Marjon Cannons (2000, as Tamar Valley Cannons)

Motorcycle Speedway Teams
Exeter Falcons (1947–2005)
Plymouth Devils (1932–70, re-formed 2006)

Devon Racecourses
Devon & Exeter. The racecourse at Kennford, south of Exeter, has provided a popular venue since the reign of Charles II. At 2 miles long and 850ft above sea level it is the second longest and highest in England.

Newton Abbot. Racing began here in 1866, but was suspended during the First and Second World Wars, being occupied by troops and used as a prisoner of war camp in the 1914–18 conflict. The main grandstand, built in 1969, was opened by Queen Elizabeth the Queen Mother.

Point-to-Point Venues
Bishops Court, near Ottery St Mary
Black Forest Lodge, near Exeter
Bratton Down, near South Molton
Buckfastleigh, Dean Court Farm
Flete, near Ivybridge
Ideford Arch, near Chudleigh
Kilworthy, near Tavistock
Stafford Cross, near Seaton
Umberleigh
Upcott Cross
Vauterhill, near Umberleigh

12

A FINAL JAUNT
AROUND THE COUNTY

During the local government reorganisation in the early 1970s which led to the creation of several new counties throughout Britain, Plymouth lobbied for the creation of a new Tamarside county to include Plymouth, Torpoint, Saltash and the rural hinterland. The campaign was unsuccessful, and on 1 April 1974 Plymouth ceased to be a county borough, with responsibility for education, social services, highways and libraries transferred to Devon County Council. These powers were restored to the city when it became a unitary authority on 1 April 1998 under the recommendations of the Banham Commission.

'Discobolos', a statue of a naked disc thrower (which with a name like that was probably asking for a vulgar nickname) which formerly stood in Rock Park, Barnstaple, was removed during the 1970s and destroyed. Some said this was as it was badly damaged and beyond repair, others that it was indecent. A former official, according to a colleague, said that those who defended it and 'showed too much interest in statues of naked men would be better off in jail'.

The Devon Rex cat breed was first discovered at Buckfastleigh in the 1960s.

On the clock face on the side of St Peter's Church, Buckland-in-the-Moor, starting at 9 o'clock, instead of numerals are letters in Gothic script, reading clockwise, 'MY DEAR MOTHER'.

Dartmoor granite taken from Haytor quarry in the nineteenth century was used in the building of London Bridge, the British

Museum and Covent Garden. The last granite quarried there prior to closure was for the Exeter War Memorial in 1919.

There are towns called Devon in Canada (in Alberta and Ontario), and in the United States of America (in Montana); and there are about 40 other Plymouths throughout the world, including about 30 in the United States alone. Others are in Nova Scotia, Canada; Montserrat, where Plymouth was the capital until abandoned in 1997 after a volcanic eruption; and New Plymouth on North Island, New Zealand. There is a Devon River in central Scotland.

J.K. Rowling, who attended Exeter University, has in the Harry Potter books a family called Weasley who live at Ottery St Catchpole, believed to be based on Ottery St Mary.

The Church of St Nectan, Hartland, sometimes called the Cathedral of North Devon, has the county's tallest church tower, 128ft. Built probably in the fourteenth century, it has also served as a navigational aid for ships.

A survey in 2006 conducted by UKTV Style Gardens channel asked for counties to be ranked according to their countryside, villages and wildlife. North Yorkshire came top of the poll with 31.3 per cent of the votes, Devon second with 21.7 per cent – comfortably

ahead of Derbyshire, third with 10 per cent. Moreover, in surveys of Britain's 50 grimmest towns and cities (oh, all right, 'Crap Towns'), based on factors such as the crime rate, unemployment and lack of facilities, those in Devon have been conspicuously absent.

The title Duke of Devonshire is held by the Cavendish family, whose estates are in Derbyshire. In medieval times the title had been held by the de Redvers family and then by the Courtenay family. William Courtenay, 1st Earl of Devon, married Princess Katherine of York, a younger daughter of King Edward IV. Their son was made Marquess of Exeter, but he was executed for treason in 1539 and his only son died in 1556, of syphilis according to some, and poisoned according to others. The latter was childless, and the peerage thus became vacant. The Cavendish family therefore chose the name of Devonshire in the English peerage as they wanted to align themselves with one of the oldest families in England, and there was already an earldom of Derby in existence.

DEVON BLUE PLAQUES

Unlike London, Devon does not have a fully coordinated system of blue plaques, but several towns and areas of the county have individual blue plaques commemorating specific people and places. The following is a selection for those to be seen in each city or town

Exmouth
Manchester House, Imperial Road, formerly home of Mary Anne Clarke, mistress to Frederick, Duke of York, second son of King George III.
Sir John Colleton, who introduced a new species of flowering shrub to England from South Carolina, *Magnolia Grandiflora Exmouthiensis*, adopted as the flower for Exmouth; he had a mansion, Elm Cottage, in Exeter Road, close to the public library. Conrad Martens, artist on the *Beagle* with Charles Darwin, who subsequently settled in Australia, also on the library.

Primrose Cottage, North Street, last remaining thatched cottage in the town centre.

Assembly Rooms, The Beacon, centre of social life in the town during the late eighteenth and early nineteenth centuries.

Manor Hotel, The Beacon, where composer Franz Liszt gave a recital in 1840.

Deer Leap, The Esplanade, nineteenth-century bath house.

Lieutenant Richard Sandford, 15 The Beacon, First World War submariner who took part in St George's Day raid on Zeebrugge.

Dolforgan Court, Louisa Terrace, home of Charlotte Anne Hume Long, founder of Exmouth's first hospital in 1884.

Tiverton

Bridge Street (No. 10), where dramatist Hannah Cowley lived from 1801 to 1809.

Fore Street and Bampton Street junction, where Lord Palmerston gave election addresses from one of the windows.

St Peter Street (Nos 48/50), where John Heathcoat, founder of the town's lace-making industry, lived from 1817 to 1832.

Torquay

The Rainbow, home of Ella Rowcroft, daughter of Sir Edward Payson Wills of Imperial Tobacco fame, she was the main contributor to the medical facilities of the English Riviera, and left her home Pilmuir in trust as a convalescent home, now Rowcroft Hospice.

Torquay Market, one of the largest and oldest in the town.

Madrepole Place, the town's first school, built in 1826.

Drum Inn, Cockington, built by Sir Edwin Lutyens and completed in 1936.

Torquay's First Methodist Church, the site of an eight-cottage terrace, two of which were used from 1807 as the first Methodist Church in the town.

Elizabeth Barrett Browning came to Torquay in 1838 to recuperate afters illness and stayed at what is today The Hotel Regina, Victoria Parade.

Cleave Court, later Riviera Court, home of writer Beverley Nichols from 1913 to 1924.

The Revd John MacEnery, brought to Torquay to be chaplain to the Cary family, first to record evidence of prehistoric man.

William Pengelly, teacher, lecturer, geologist and philanthropist, who spent fifteen years excavating Kents Cavern.

Orestone, home of John Calcott Horsley, brother-in-law to Isambard K. Brunel, artist and designer of the world's first Christmas card.

Abbey Hall, Torquay's first grammar school, originally opened as a Teachers' Centre in 1904.

Meadfoot House, Hesketh Crescent, leased to Charles Darwin and his family during the summer of 1861.

Paignton

Bijou Theatre, famous for the world premiere of Gilbert and Sullivan's *The Pirates of Penzance*, plaque on the side of Hyde Road (see p. 27).

Oldway Mansion, former home of Washington M. Singer, of the Singer sewing machine family. Built in about 1870 as a private residence, Steartfield House, Steartfield Road, became the family home of Washington, second son of Isaac, founder of the Singer Sewing Machine Company, rebuilt by his third son Paris Singer in the style of the Palace at Versailles.

Primley House, home of Herbert Whitley, founder of Paignton Zoo.

Redcliffe, once home of Col Robert Smith, who had a vision for Redcliffe, completed in 1864 and today is the Redcliffe Hotel on Paignton's seafront. This unique building has a tunnel to the beach.

Bishops Place Cottages, built by I.K. Brunel to house his railway company doctor, engineer, architect/surveyor and chief buyer. The doctor was based at No. 1 and 150 years on it is still a medical practice.

Brixham

Berry Head House, home of the Revd Henry Lyte, Vicar of All Saints Church, who wrote 'Abide with Me' (see pp. 25–6). The house is now the Berry Head Hotel.

Vale House, Galmpton, home of Robert Graves, novelist and poet, in the Second World War.

Berry Head Road, where Sir James Callaghan, former Prime
   Minister, lived as a boy in the 1920s when his father was a
   coastguard in the town.

Tavistock
The Tavy Foundry
Victorian Cemetery
Pannier Market
Bedford Hotel
Guildhall
Bedford Hotel
Ordulph Arms

Dartmouth
Theodore Veale, Royal Avenue Gardens, Victoria Cross winner
   for most conspicuous bravery during the Battle of the Somme,
   1916.
John Davis, explorer (see p. 171), Dartmouth Quay.
Dartmouth Castle, fortalice, or remains of a fourteenth-century
   curtain wall and tower from a small fort.
Flora Thompson, Lauriston, on the house where she came to
   stay in 1940 and completed her novels *Over to Candleford*,
   Candleford Green and *Still Glides the Stream.*

Exeter
Peter Hennis (see p. 63), plaque outside the graveyard at Sidwell Street, where he is buried.
W.G. Hoskins (see p. 49), plaque on the house at St David's Hill, where he was born.

Budleigh Salterton
Sir John Everett Millais, The Octagon, on a house where he stayed in 1870 while painting 'The Boyhood of Raleigh'.

Sidmouth
Beach House
Royal York Hotel
Sidmouth Lifeboat Station

Plymouth
Captain F.J. Walker, Hoegate Street, Captain in the Royal Navy, reckoned as most successful anti-submarine warfare commander during the Battle of the Atlantic.

TWELVE MAJOR BOOKS ABOUT DEVON

Of the wealth of titles written and published about the county, these twelve titles published during the last half century on various aspects should provide a comprehensive and reasonably up-to-date guide.

Burton, S.H., *Devon Villages*, Robert Hale, 1973
Burton, S.H., *Exmoor*, Robert Hale, 1974
Gill, Crispin, *Plymouth: A New History*, Devon Books, 1993
Goodall, Felicity, *Lost Devon*, Birlinn, 2007
Gordon, D. St Leger, *Devon*, Robert Hale, 1977

Harris, Helen, *Industrial Archaeology of Dartmoor*, David & Charles, 1968

Hemery, Eric, *High Dartmoor*, David & Charles, 1983

Hoskins, W.G., *Devon*, Devon Books, 1992

Le Messurier, Brian, *Dartmoor Artists*, Halsgrove, 2002

Lethbridge, Tony, *Exeter: History and Guide*, Tempus, 2005

Minchinton, W.E., *Devon at Work*, David & Charles, 1974

Stanes, Robin, *A History of Devon*, Phillimore, 1986

Also by the same author

Devon Murders

Devonshire's Own

A Grim Almanac of Devon

Plymouth History & Guide

More Devon Murders

Plymouth Book of Days

Visit our website and discover thousands of other
History Press books.

www.thehistorypress.co.uk